Typographic Insights

Articles on
Understanding & Using Type

Part Two

H. Carl Shank

CARE Typography

Typographic Insights: Articles on Understanding & Using Type, Part Two

About the Author

Carl Shank is a layout and type designer having started with IBM Selectric Composers and phototypesetters in the early 1980s and then Apple LaserWriters in 1985 and beyond in addition to his pastoral and theological work. He worked for a regular Washington D.C. area print shop heading up the typesetting and layout department in the early 1980s.

Carl designed an initial Greek font for the Zondervan Corporation in the early 1990s and has worked with his own company, CARE Typography, since the late 1980s. He has developed an appreciation for not merely the mechanics of good typesetting and layout work, but also the fine art of the craft of typesetting.

These articles are from his website, *caretypography.com*, in the BLOG section of the site. He is grateful for all the professional typesetters and designers who have offered assistance over the years and submit this booklet as a summary of best typesetting and layout practices that he has gleaned from many experts in the fields of printing and typesetting.

cshanktype@gmail.com
www.carlshankconsulting.com
www.caretypography.com

Table of Contents

Part Two

Foreword

I learned about type and typesetting and printing the hard way. I am by training and trade most of my life a pastor and theologian who ministers in many different ways to people and churches. I do consulting work with leaders and their churches.

What all of this has to do with typography is a story in and of itself. In my ministerial journey, I served with many different sized churches and congregational needs. That included finding a part-time job to supplement my ministerial income. Such a job came to me in a commercial print shop in northern Virginia in the 1980s. I must admit I fell in love with typography there and everything involved in the planning and preparation of printed materials. So, I was schooled by the printers and typesetters there and learned the business.

When Apple Computer back in the mid-1980s introduced the Macintosh and the LaserWriter with the promise of in-home layout and acceptable typesetting with programs like PageMaker, I was hooked. I began a business on the side called CARE Typography. I began producing simple layout jobs for church folks and then for community people and businesses I got to know.

My love for typesetting grew to the point of type designing, and a major Christian book company hired me to do a Greek typeface for them. This was daunting work, no doubt, but with the help of typeface designers I got to know, most of the typeface was designed by me for this company. I had to pass the finishing touches of the face onto another much more experienced designer since my church position changed and I had to place a priority on that.

But my love for typography continued to grow and develop. Reading and taking online instruction have helped me develop myself as a self-trained and proficient typographer, though not by any means a professional. I offer this book, therefore, as someone who has come up through the ranks of printing and typesetting. This book is a second in a series of typographic articles. It is from a number of additional website blogs that I have written for *caretypography.com* since the first edition.

I obviously have depended on many professional typesetters and authors of the craft of typography. My special thanks to Robert Bringhurst, *The Elements of Typographic Style* for many of my notes and insights.[1] Credit is also due to Stephen Coles, *The Anatomy of Type: A Graphic Guide to 100 Typefaces,* Kindle Edition; Philip Brady, *Using Type Right: 121 Basic No-Nonsense Rules for Working With Type* (Northlight, 1998); Stephen Moye, *Fontographer: Type By Design* (MIS Press, 1995) and many other online sources.

My hope and desire is that this little book is an encouragement to all those desktop publishing and typographic people just trying to navigate the often complex waters of typography and printing.

Carl Shank
Fall 2023

Notes

1.   Robert Bringhurst, *The Elements of Typographic Style,* Version 3.1 (Vancouver, B.C., 1992, 1996, 2004, 2005).

A note about fine typography: The text of this book is set generally with the typeface Arno Pro, in Regular, Italic and Bold, 12 on 16 point, with opening quotes and endnotes set at 10/12. The versals or leading capital letters are Arno Pro Bold Display, 14/16. Most of the interior type has been set using Adobe InDesign 2023/4 with justification controls set as below for evenness of text:

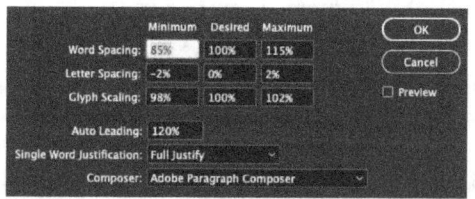

New Font Offerings

Two New Fonts

"Fontographer is not just for alphabets. You are probably aware of fonts
such as Hermann Zapf's Dingbats but might not be aware of
Richard Beatty's needle-point font. Each letter represents
a different color of thread . . . or Judith Sutcliffe's charming
Petroglph Hawaii."
(Stephen Moye, *Fontographer: Type By Design*)

Introducing the Christograph Font and Fanciful Alphabets Font. CARE Typography is pleased to announce two new font offerings, especially for use in churches and ministries—the Christograph Font and the Fanciful Alphabets Font. These are pictograph fonts, designed from pictograms courtesy of *The Image Book: 2,500 Visual and Verbal Images to Clip and Use During the Church Year* (C.I. Publishing, 1993).

The pictograms used have been cleanly drawn and sized to fit a normal sized font display. There are 83 pictograms in the Christograph font that occupy font glyphs. They cover the church year adequately and can be used in a variety of newsletter and display materials. These fonts are true Open Type Postscript fonts, the kind preferred by Adobe systems.

The Fanciful Alphabets Font is a decorative capital letter font, from A to Z, suitable for fancy text introductions or stand alone old time graphics. One of the nice things about having such fancy lettering in a font family is that they can be sized to fit most any text or advertising use, especially in the larger sizes.

The fonts are free to all churches and ministries. To secure your copy of the fonts, send an email to CARE Typography at cshanktype@gmail.com. The fonts are copyrighted by CARE Typography and can be used only by permission from the creator.

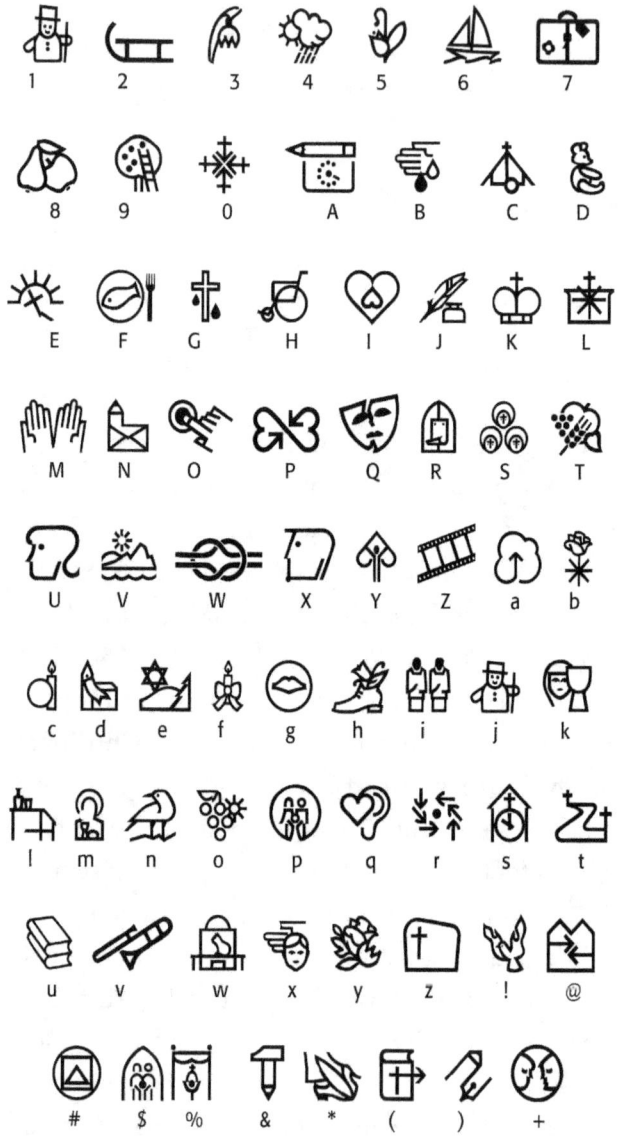

; : , < . > / ?

x

A number of Pictograms used in the typeface construction
courtesy of *The Image Book: 2,500 Visual and Verbal Images
to Clip and Use During the Church Year* (C. I. Publishing,
1993). Used by permission for church and non-profits.
Fontographer 5 used for typeface creation.

CARE Typography
A Division of
Carl Shank Consulting
374 Alexandria Ct
Marietta, PA 17547
717.385.6468
cshanktype@gmail.com
carl@carlshankconsulting.com

Websites
carlshankconsulting.com
caretypography.com

TYPE CHART
Christograph Font

KEY	CHAR	Shift CHAR	Option CHAR	Shift Option CHAR	KEY	CHAR	Shift CHAR	Option CHAR	Shift Option CHAR
A	⌂	⌂			Y	❀	♠		
B	❀	❧			Z	⊡	⊟		
C	♪	⚒			1	⚑	❦		
D	⌂	⚖			2	⊏	⌂		
E	⚘	☀			3	◉	◎		
F	⚱	◑			4	☁	⌂		
G	⊖	✝			5	✌	⊟		
H	⚘	✿			6	⛵			
I	⚐	♡			7	⊡	⊤		
J	⚱	✎			8	◍	⚒		
K	⊡	♛			9	◉	⊞		
L	⌂	⊞			0	✦	∿		
M	⊡	⚬			!	✿			
N	⊿	✉			-	⌂			
O	❀	⚒			=	⚑	◉		
P	◉	⚭			×	⚘			
Q	♡	⊡			;	⊡	⊡		
R	❀	⌂			,	⊤	✿		
S	⌂	⚬			.	⊷	☀		
T	⚒	⚘			/	⌇	⚬		
U	⊟	⊂			—	⚱			
V	⚒	⚘							
W	⊡	⊷							
X	❀	⌂			space bar				

12

TYPE CHART
Christograph Font KEY

1 = January	g = Group
2 = February	h = Hiking
3 = March	i = Assistants
4 = April	j = January
5 = May	k = Confirmation
6 = June	l = Lecture
7 = July	m = Maundy Thursday
8 = August	n = November
9 = September	o = October
0 = Ecumenical	p = Parents
A = Appointments	q = Confession
B = Baptism	r = Recycle
C = Camp	s = Schedule
D = Daycare	t = Stations of Cross
E = Easter	u = Book
F = Fasting	v = Brass
G = Good Friday	w = Winter
H = Handicap	x = Confirmation Boy
I = Intercession	y = Congratulations
J = Journal	z = Cemetery
K = King	! = Pentecost
L = Liturgy	# = Contemplation
M = Meditation	$ = Contemporary
N = Newsletter	% = Corpus
O = Office	& = Crafts
P = Parish	* = Dance
Q = Ash Wednesday	+ = Discussion
R = Reformation	< = Fall
S = Saints	> = Summer
T = Thanksgiving	= = School Start
U = Women	? = Seniors
V = Vacation	@ = Social
W = Wedding	: = Slides
X = Men	; = Study
Y = Youth	, = Procession
Z = Movie	- = Radio (dash)
a = Ascension	/ = Passion
b = Birthday	. = Penance
c = Communion	— = Pilgrim (minus sign)
d = Dedication	(= Evangelism
e = Epiphany	) = Education
f = First Communion	× = Spring (multiplication)

Fanciful Alphabets Font

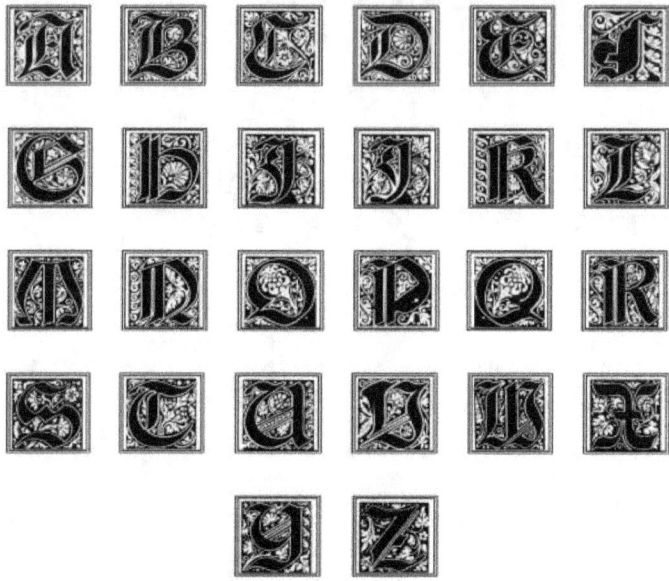

0 1 2 3 4 5 6 7 8 9

FancifulAlphabets Font

 nce upon a time a brother and sister named Hansel and Gretel lived in a hut in the woods with their father. Their father was a poor woodcutter. His wife, their mother, had died when the two children were very young. Their father thought he would not be lonely anymore when he finally re-married. But the new

Fancy Drop Caps

Versals

"Another excellent method of marking the start of the text,
inherited from ancient scribal practice, is a large initial capital:
a versal or lettrine."
(Robert Bringhurst, *The Elements of Typographic Style*)

Drop caps, or technically, versals, are larger letters that mark the start of a major text block. They are often larger than the surrounding text and visibly show off the start of a major textual work. Typographers use drop caps, often for fun and visual appeal, to show off their skill and visual intuition. Drop caps herald back to letterpress and scribal tradition, with many of them coming from calligraphy.

The practice of using drop caps dates back to the medieval times when scribes would embellish the first letter of a manuscript to make it stand out and emphasize its importance. In the early days of printing, drop caps were used primarily for their aesthetic value. Printers would carve elaborate woodcut or metal typefaces to create intricate and ornate drop caps that would catch the reader's eye and add visual interest to the page. Drop caps were often used in religious texts, where they were seen as a way to honor the divine word.

Over time, drop caps became more standardized and simpler in design, but they continued to be used as a way to add visual interest and hierarchy to the page. They were commonly used in books, newspapers, and magazines to indicate the beginning of a new section or chapter, or to draw attention to a particularly important paragraph or quote. In the digital age, drop caps have remained popular and are used in a wide range of documents, including books, magazines, newsletters, and websites. While digital drop caps lack the intricate detail and texture of their printed counterparts, they can still be effective in adding visual interest and emphasis.

Adobe has a new program for creating text based images, called Adobe Firefly. The final display below is a sampling of text made into complex images using this new program. It is an exciting program for graphic artists and designers and even typographers looking for eye-catching display.

I have included below some fancy drop caps and how they might be used in a text opening. Enjoy!

FANCY DROP CAP FONTS
with Descriptions & Uses

ART Nouveau Caps • 60 pt

Floral Caps Nouveau • 60 pt

Botanic Personal • 60 pt

FancifulAlphabet • 60 pt

AnnStone • 60 pt

Fette Fraktur • 60 pt

Cottonwood • 60 pt

𝔄 𝔅 ℭ 𝔇 𝔈

Blackletter • 60 pt

A B C D E

Engravers Old English • 60 pt

A B C D E

Blackriver • 60 pt

Kramer • 60 pt

nce upon a time a brother and sister named Hansel and Gretel lived in a hut in the woods with their father. Their father was a poor woodcutter. His wife, their mother, had died when the two children were very young. Their father thought he would not be lonely anymore when he finally re-married. But the new

Art Nouveau Caps

Inspired by the international art movement that emerged at the end of the 19th century and reached its peak between 1890 and 1910. It was a reaction against the traditional academic art of the time, which was seen as too rigid and formulaic, and sought to create a new style that was more organic, expressive, and individualistic.

nce upon a time a brother and sister named Hansel and Gretel lived in a hut in the woods with their father. Their father was a poor woodcutter. His wife, their mother, had died when the two children were very young. Their father thought he would not be lonely anymore when he finally re-married. But the new

Floral Caps Nouveau

Inspired by the international art movement that emerged at the end of the 19th century and reached its peak between 1890 and 1910. It was a reaction against the traditional academic art of the time, which was seen as too rigid and formulaic, and sought to create a new style that was more organic, expressive, and individualistic.

DSType Ver 1.1
Copyright © Typographer Mediengestaltung, 2000.
All rights reserved.

nce upon a time a brother and sister named Hansel and Gretel lived in a hut in the woods with their father. Their father was a poor woodcutter. His wife, their mother, had died when the two children were very young. Their father thought he would not be lonely anymore when he finally re-married. But the new

Botanic Personal Use Bold

Billy Argel
https://billyargel.com/
Copyright © 2021 by Billy Argel. All rights reserved.
PERSONAL USE ONLY! Commercial licenses and complete set available @ https://billyargel.com/ More infos contact @ https://billyargel.com/contact-us/

nce upon a time a brother and sister named Hansel and Gretel lived in a hut in the woods with their father. Their father was a poor woodcutter. His wife, their mother, had died when the two children were very young. Their father thought he would not be lonely anymore when he finally re-married. But the new

FancifulAlphabets Font

The FancifulAlphabets Font is a decorative capital letter font, from A to Z, suitable for fancy text introductions or stand alone old time graphics. One of the nice things about having such fancy lettering in a font family is that they can be sized to fit most any text or advertising use, especially in the larger sizes. Inspired by *The Image Book: 2,500 Visual and Verbal Images to Clip and Use During the Church Year* (C.I. Publishing, 1993).

nce upon a time a brother and sister named Hansel and Gretel lived in a hut in the woods with their father. Their father was a poor woodcutter. His wife, their mother, had died when the two children were very young. Their father thought he would not be lonely anymore when he finally re-married. But the new

AnnStone

Note the subtle background of the lettering. This would also be an art nouveau offering.

nce upon a time a brother and sister named Hansel and Gretel lived in a hut in the woods with their father. Their father was a poor woodcutter. His wife, their mother, had died when the two children were very young. Their father thought he would not be lonely anymore when he finally re-married. But the new

Fette Fraktur

Fette Fraktur is a blackletter typeface of the sub-classification Fraktur designed by the German punchcutter Johann Christian Bauer (1802–1867) in 1850. The C.E. Weber Foundry published a version in 1875, and the D Stempel AG foundry published the version shown at right in 1908.

nce upon a time a brother and sister named Hansel and Gretel lived in a hut in the woods with their father. Their father was a poor woodcutter. His wife, their mother, had died when the two children were very young. Their father thought he would not be lonely anymore when he finally re-married. But the new

Cottonwood

Cottonwood is an Adobe Originals typeface designed in 1991 by Kim Buker Chansler, Barbara Lind, and Joy Redick. Note the Texas,cowboy-like design.

Once upon a time a brother and sister named Hansel and Gretel lived in a hut in the woods with their father. Their father was a poor woodcutter. His wife, their mother, had died when the two children were very young. Their father thought he would not be lonely anymore when he finally re-married. But the new

Blackletter

Blackletter, also called Gothic script or Old English script, in calligraphy, a style of alphabet that was used for manuscript books and documents throughout Europe—especially in German-speaking countries—from the end of the 12th century to the 20th century.

Fontographer 4.1. 2002
©2002 by Andrew Leman. www.ahleman.com
www.cthulhulives.org

Once upon a time a brother and sister named Hansel and Gretel lived in a hut in the woods with their father. Their father was a poor woodcutter. His wife, their mother, had died when the two children were very young. Their father thought he would not be lonely anymore when he finally re-married. But the new

Engravers Old English

Engravers Old English is a plain, sturdy rendition of the blackletter style, commonly known as Old English. It was designed in 1901 by Morris Benton and another person identified by ATF only as Cowan, but has also been ascribed to Joseph W. Phinney.

Once upon a time a brother and sister named Hansel and Gretel lived in a hut in the woods with their father. Their father was a poor woodcutter. His wife, their mother, had died when the two children were very young. Their father thought he would not be lonely anymore when he finally re-married. But the new

Blackriver

Blackriver is a Vintage Font inspired by vintage packaging and advertising from the early 20th century. It is perfect for vintage logo design, headlines or packaging design. The product also includes a set of floral vector illustrations as well as some decorative ornaments.

Once upon a time a brother and sister named Hansel and Gretel lived in a hut in the woods with their father. Their father was a poor woodcutter. His wife, their mother, had died when the two children were very young. Their father thought he would not be lonely anymore when he finally re-married. But the new

Kramer

Kramer is an Art Nouveau drop cap font with the letter outlines themselves cut out to form the lower case letters. Again, note the intertwining vine background, typical of art nouveau.

DSType Ver 1.2

Adobe Firefly (Beta)

These four (4) drop caps are actually images created in the new Adobe Firefly (Beta) program. They adhere to strict standards of "content credentials" drafted by Adobe and others for use of AI generated images. Image 1 is a garden flower hibiscus display. Image 2 is called "driftwood." Image 3 is "denim jeans," and image 4 is "leafy pothos." The base text used is Alfam2, placed in Adobe InDesign with a circular text wrap.

O nce upon a time a brother and sister named Hansel and Gretel lived in a hut in the woods with their father. Their father was a poor woodcutter. His wife, their mother, had died when the two children were very young. Their father thought he would not be lonely anymore when he finally re-married. But the new

O nce upon a time a brother and sister named Hansel and Gretel lived in a hut in the woods with their father. Their father was a poor woodcutter. His wife, their mother, had died when the two children were very young. Their father thought he would not be lonely anymore when he finally re-married. But the new nce upon a time a brother and sister named Hansel and Gretel lived in a hut in the woods with their father. Their father was a poor woodcutter. His wife, their mother, had died when the two children were very young. Their father thought he would not be lonely anymore when he finally re-married. But the new

nce upon a time a brother and sister named Hansel and Gretel lived in a hut in the woods with their father. Their father was a poor woodcutter. His wife, their mother, had died when the two children were very young. Their father thought he would not be lonely anymore when he finally re-married. But

nce upon a time a brother and sister named Hansel and Gretel lived in a hut in the woods with their father. Their father was a poor woodcutter. His wife, their mother, had died when the two children were very young. Their father thought he would not be lonely anymore when he finally re-married.

Decluttering A Layout

Hardware Store Ad Do Over

"Every consumer is a bundle of contradictions. When shopping
we want to feel carefree and spontaneous. At the same time
we want to know that the provider is competent, stable and secure.
Freedom and limitations, all at once!"
(Nigel French & Hugh D'Andrade, *The Type Project Book*)

We have a wonderful hometown hardware store that has been in operation for many years. Rather than going to a big box store, many choose this hometown hardware store for everything from a screw to a refrigerator or mower. They advertise frequently in our hometown newspaper.

Some time ago, I found an ad for mowers from the store. It looked clunky and not very clear or inviting. How do you go about de-cluttering or revamping a busy image? The image below was a local ad for a hardware store emphasizing lawn work equipment. The type should be easy to read and the graphics and fonts used should enhance the theme of the ad. I find the original ad "clunky" and hard to decipher what is really important. Is it the hardware store? Is it the lawn equipment? Is it the emphasis on servicing the local communities for quite some time?

One major problem is using fonts that are sized incorrectly for the ad to stand out to the viewer. The remade ad uses a family of fonts, namely Avenir Next Condensed in various styles. Using the same font clarifies and highlights rather than obscures the message of the flyer. While the revamped flyer is limited to one major font style, you can generally use as many as three fonts in a publication to keep it from being cluttered. Because of the variety of font styles in the Avenir Next family, we can have both display fonts and text fonts from the same basic font family.

About those graphics. The graphics chosen to illustrate lawn equipment are scattered, not sharp, and stand in contention with the companies advertised — Toro, Echo, Husqvarna and Troy-Bilt. Are we supposed to focus on the companies or the products of these companies? That is unclear. The store Hostetter logo is indeed central to the ad, but the hours of operation are not emphasized. I suppose the yellow marker used is suppose to highlight those times as well as long standing service to the community.

The point in a display ad such as this one is to increase readability and invite the reader to investigate what is being offered. The revamped ad does this in a clean and clear way.

Type For Text

Clear and Legible Text Type

"Typography is about making something a bit more readable
for a bit less money. When type makes timetables and
newspapers easier to read, it improves the quality of life
by that much."
(Mike Parker)

Type for text. What type do you use for regular text, such as in books, articles, reports, proposals and the like? A number of typographers and writers throughout history have settled on actually a few few faces that make it to the top of the list for typing regular text. I have noted them and written about them in the graphics below.

Some very favorite type for text faces include Adobe Caslon, Adobe Garamond, Janson Text, and Times New Roman, all of which have been faithfully used throughout the history of book making. Designed by Robert Slimbach, Arno Pro (used in this book) is also a favorite face of mine that I have used in a number of books I have written. I find the face inviting, clear, very readable and legible and dense enough and comfortable enough for any reader.

Myfonts.com notes this about the Arno font — "Named after the Florentine river which runs through the heart of the Italian Renaissance, Arno draws on the warmth and readability of early humanist typefaces of the 15th and 16th centuries. While inspired by the past, Arno is distinctly contemporary in both appearance and function. Designed by Adobe Principal Designer Robert Slimbach, Arno is a meticulously-crafted face in the tradition of early Venetian and Aldine book typefaces. Embodying themes Slimbach has explored in typefaces such as Minion and Brioso,

Arno represents a distillation of his design ideals and a refinement of his craft. As a multi-featured OpenType family, with the most extensive Latin-based glyph complement Adobe has yet offered, Arno offers extensive pan-European language support, including Cyrillic and polytonic Greek. The family also offers such typographic niceties as five optical size ranges, extensive swash italic sets, and small capitals for all covered languages."

What makes a font a good and highly usable text font? John McWade in his expertly written and illustrated *Before & After Magazine* series, said it well — "The hallmarks of good text type are legibility and readability. Legibility refers to clarity; it's how readily one letter can be distinguished from all others. Readability refers to how well letters interact to compose words, sentences and paragraphs. When evaluating the choices,, your operative word is medium." (John McWade, *Before & After*, Vol. 4. No. 3. 1994)

Medium fonts include fonts with medium x-height, that is the height of a lowercase letter of a typeface, fonts with medium height-to-width ratio in the individual letters, that is, letters that do not look distorted or weirdly shaped, and fonts with some variability in stroke weights that distinguish each letter from its neighbors. The latter description leads us away from too uniform geometric sans-serif styles and beautiful, super thin strokes of some modern styles of fonts.

The fonts I have chosen, with help from McWade and others, are great text fonts. They show up well in text heavy applications. I have included some of the history of the font in the ones chosen below. In addition to the faces mentioned above, I have included Stone Serif, a relatively modern face, and Bembo, a stylish face for some jobs. Use these time tested fonts for your heavy text work, and you will not be disappointed.

Adobe Caslon

Sample Text Bold
Sample Text Semibold
Sample Text Italic

Aspeliquia dis es et qui doluptat ma as rerrumque vero bero eum alitatem quia venis est fugit etur? destore non nis autecaectis reribus andebiste ne veliae veliatiae mos eariore mporrumquas escium fugiteculpa dolorporepe voluptae cuptibus.

Font: Adobe Caslon Pro, 12/14

Faces: Regular, *Italic*, Semibold, *Semibold Italic*, **Bold**, ***Bold Italic***

Creator: Carol Twombly 1989 based on faces cut by William Caslon, London, 1730s. Revival of Baroque typefaces.

Italic: *True Italic, 20° angle*

Special Letters: Text figures, SMALL CAPS, good fraction selection, ligatures, ornaments ▧ ❀ ⅏

Legibility: Safe, solid, dependable

Readability: Comfortable, easy to read

Beauty: Average

Adobe Caslon: Identifying Characteristics

A C *v w*

Note the scooped out top of the capital "A," the double serifs on the capital "C," and the swashed ;ower case "v" and "w" in the italic face. "Caslon's roman became so popular that it was known as the script of kings, although on the other side of the political spectrum (and the ocean), the Americans used it for their Declaration of Independence in 1776. The original Caslon specimen sheets and punches have long provided a fertile source for the range of types bearing his name."

(Description from myfonts.com)

Adobe Garamond

Sample Text
Sample Text Bold
Sample Text Italic

Aspeliquia dis es et qui doluptat ma as rerrumque vero bero eum alitatem quia venis est fugit etur? destore non nis autecaectis reribus andebiste ne veliae veliatiae mos eariore mporrumquas escium eseque magnia id que nonse culpari qui as dit fugiteculpa dolorporepe voluptae cuptibus.

Font: Adobe Garamond Pro, 12/14

Faces: Regular, *Italic*, **Bold**, **Bold Italic**

Creator: Robert Slimbach, 1989, after Claude Garamond, Paris, c. 1540. High Renaissance forms, humanist (oblique) axis. Revival of Baroque typefaces.

Italic: *True Italic*

Special Variations: Stempel Garamond, Granjon, ITC Garamond in the 1970s

Legibility: Also a fine display face

Readability: Can be set at 10 point minimum

Beauty: Elegant

Adobe Garamond: Identifying Characteristics

Q&4$MGTR?
ozrfg

Garamond is elegant, refined and speaks of French refinery, being designed in sixteenth century Paris and "owes much to Italian forms and belongs to the world of Renaissance Catholicism. Renaissance letterforms are full of sensuous and unhurried light and space. They have served as typographic benchmarks for five hundred years." Also serves as a fine display face.

(Description from Robert Bringhurst, *The Elements of Typographic Style*, Vers. 3.1, Hartley & Marks, 1992, 1996, 2004, 2005)

Bembo

Sample Text

Sample Text Bold

Sample Text Extra Bold

Sample Text Italic

Aspeliquia dis es et qui doluptat ma as rerrumque vero bero eum alitatem quia venis est fugit etur? destore non nis autecaectis reribus andebiste ne veliae veliatiae mos eariore mporrumquas dit fugiteculpa dolorporepe voluptae cuptibus.

Font: Bembo Regular, 12/14

Faces: Regular, *Italic,* Semibold, **Bold,** ***Bold Italic,*** **Extra Bold**

Creator: Francesco Griffo in 1496 and this was released by Monotype Imaging by Stanley Morison, 1929

Italic: *True Italic*

Special Variations: 31 weights, including small caps, Old style figures, expert characters, and an alternate cap R

Legibility: Very readable but too stylish for some

Readability: Book typography and **heavier weights in ads**

Beauty: Dependability

Bembo: Identifying Characteristics

Q&4$MGTR?
qzrfg

The Bembo design was named after notable the Venetian poet, Cardinal and literary theorist of the 16th century Pietro Bembo. The typeface originally used to publish Pietro Bembo's book *De Aetna,* a book about Bembo's visit to Mount Etna. The Bembo typeface was cut by Francesco Griffo, a Venetian goldsmith who had become a punchcutter and worked for revered printer Aldus Manutius. It was adapted later by Stanley Morison at Monotype. The italic is based on letters cut by the Renaissance scribe Giovanni Tagliente. The lighter weights of Bembo are popular for book typography. The heavier weights impart a look of conservative dependability to advertising and packaging projects, such as Heathrow Airport in London.

(Description from myfonts.com, freefontsfamily.com, and dfonts.org)

Janson Text

Sample Text
Sample Text Bold
Sample Text Bold Italic
Sample Text Italic

Aspeliquia dis es et qui doluptat ma as rerrumque vero bero eum alitatem quia venis est fugit etur? destore non nis autecaectis reribus andebiste ne veliae veliatiae mos eariore mporrumquas escium eseque magnia id voluptae cuptibus.

Font: Janson Text, 12/14

Faces: Regular, *Italic*, **Bold**, ***Bold Italic***

Creator: Miklós Kis, Amsterdam, about 1685. A revival of Baroque typefaces.

Italic: *True Italic 56*

Special Variations: 2 weights plus italics. Only the Roman has SMALL CAPS, Latin glyphs included in the Arabic fonts.

Legibility: Extremely readable

Readability: Denseness makes for good book typography

Beauty: "Chiseled resolute appearance"

Janson Text: Identifying Characteristics

Q&4$MGTR?
qzrfg

Linotype Janson, adapted by Zapf in 1954, from the seventeenth-century originals of Miklós Kis. Linotype's digital version known as Janson Text was made under the direction of Horst Heiderhoff in 1985 [Linotype] in consultation with Adrian Frutiger and is based on Stempel's original 14-point hand-cast types of 1919 [Wallis 1990]. "Janson holds the middle ground between the earthy, workmanlike nature of Caslon and the high classiness of Garamond. Rounder and denser, it has a chiseled, resolute appearance."

(Description from John McWade, *Before & After Magazine*, Vol. 4, No. 3, 1994 as well as Robert Bringhurst, fontsinuse.com and myfonts.com)

Times New Roman

Sample Text
Sample Text Bold
Sample Text Bold Italic
Sample Text Italic

Aspeliquia dis es et qui doluptat ma as rerrumque vero bero eum alitatem quia venis est fugit etur? destore non nis autecaectis reribus andebiste ne veliae veliatiae mos eariore mporrumquas escium eseque magnia id que voluptae cuptibus.

Font: Times New Roman, 12/14

Faces: Regular, *Italic*, **Bold**, ***Bold Italic***

Creator: Stanley Morison, Victor Lardent, Victor Lardent and published by Monotype

Italic: *True Italic*

Special Variations: 12 styles plus standard Times with 4 weights, Times Ten and Times Eighteen variations

Legibility: Office ready readable

Readability: Magazine and Book type since the 1940s

Beauty: Like "a Navy blazer, always acceptable" (McWade)

Times New Roman: Identifying Characteristics

Q&4$MGTR? qzrfg

"In 1931, The Times of London commissioned a new text type design from Stanley Morison and the Monotype Corporation, after Morison had written an article criticizing The Times for being badly printed and typographically behind the times. The new design was supervised by Stanley Morison and drawn by Victor Lardent, an artist from the advertising department of The Times. Morison used an older typeface, Plantin, as the basis for his design, but made revisions for legibility and economy of space (always important concerns for newspapers). As the old type used by the newspaper had been called Times Old Roman," Morison's revision became "Times New Roman." The Times of London debuted the new typeface in October 1932, and after one year the design was released for commercial sale. The Linotype version, called simply "Times," was optimized for line-casting technology, though the differences in the basic design are subtle. The typeface was very successful for the Times of London, which used a higher grade of newsprint than most newspapers. The better, whiter paper enhanced the new typeface's high degree of contrast and sharp serifs, and created a sparkling, modern look. In 1972, Walter Tracy designed Times Europa for The Times of London. This was a sturdier version, and it was needed to hold up to the newest demands of newspaper printing: faster presses and cheaper paper. In the United States, the Times font family has enjoyed popularity as a magazine and book type since the 1940s. Times continues to be very popular around the world because of its versatility and readability. And because it is a standard font on most computers and digital printers, it has become universally familiar as the office workhorse."

(Description from myfonts.com)

Using Open Type Fonts
Highly Functional Modern Fonts*

"Open Type fonts have a larger glyph limit,
an advance over the traditional 256 glyphs in a
standard Type 1 or TrueType font."
(Adobe)

Most modern fonts are what we call "Open Type" fonts (See my Blog Post "More About Fonts"). The advantages of Open Type fonts are mainly fourfold — (1) they have a larger glyph limit (usually about 65,000 glyphs). This is an advance over the traditional 256 glyphs in a standard Type 1 or TrueType font. (2) They are cross platform fonts, thus able to be used in both Mac and Windows applications. (3) They offer support for both PostScript Type 1 and True Type outlines. (4) They support advanced typographic features. More on this later.

Open Type fonts can contain many thousands of characters and multiple alphabets, such as Latin, Greek, and Cyrillic; or Kanji, Kana, and Romaji for Japanese use. OpenType fonts can also include typographic refinements such as true small caps, different styles of figures, and extensive sets of ligatures and alternates, as well as complete sets of accented characters and diacritical marks. Different applications have differing levels of support for all the OpenType features. However, not all programs can support all Open Type features, as shown by the Windows fraction 3/16 in Microsoft Word in the Windows font Book Antiqua Sample below.

Open Type options built into advanced programs, such as Adobe InDesign and Photoshop CC include several features, that can be turned on in the "Character" menu under InDesign (See Sample Below).

Ligatures — Ligatures are typographic combinations of two or more letters into a single character (See Sample Below). There are three types of Ligatures, Standard, Discretionary and Historical. You are most likely familiar with Standard Ligatures, such as the combination of "f" plus "l" in fl or "f" plus "f" plus "i" in ffi.

Discretionary ligatures are decorative in nature, adding a unique visual element to text that does not affect its readability nor functionality (See Sample Below). Historical Ligatures maintain old-fashioned letter combinations, used for centuries by typographers, such as the combination œ ("o" plus "e") seen in medieval manuscripts. Actually, this lexical ligature is called an "ethel" and typographically required for deliberate archaism and for academically correct quotation from older English sources, as well as in some French phrases, such as *hors d'œuvre*.

Contextual Alternates — Contextual alternates are ligatures that are applied to individual characters based on the letters around them (their context). Contextual alternates can also be applied to entire words in certain contexts, for example, words frequently used in titles (such as "of" and "the"). When contextual alternates are enabled for a font, they are used instead of the standard ligatures in those contexts defined by the font designer. In Microsoft Word, contextual alternates can be found in the Open Type Features group, "Advanced" tab, on the "Font" dialogue.

Discretionary Ligatures — Discretionary ligatures are designed to be ornamental and not specifically designed for readability. They are not common in use. Texts usually borrow some of their elements as accents.

Swashes — (See Example Below) A swash is a typographical flourish, such as an exaggerated serif, terminal, tail, entry stroke, etc., on a glyph. The use of swash characters dates back to at least the 16th century, as they can be seen in Ludovico Vicentino degli Arrighi's La Operina, which is dated 1522.

Stylistic Alternates — Stylistic alternates, or simply "alternates," usually placed in one of the stylistic set features (ss01 - ss20), are usually simple one-to-one substitutions (no context) and, of course off, by default. The user can enable them.

Titling Alternates — These are specially-designed capitals that are intended for display usage. Titling characters differ from their text counterparts in that their scale, proportion and design details have been altered to look best at larger sizes.

Ordinals — In common (rather than mathematical) usage, ordinals are superscripted letters following a number, such as in 1st, 2nd and 3rd. They are used in other languages as well, for example, the Spanish and Portuguese "a" and "o" ordinals. (See Sample Below)

Fractions — Fractions can be divided into three categories–basic, extended and arbitrary. Basic fractions are ¼, ½ and ¾, and are standard in many fonts in all formats. Extended fractions are found in many, but not all, OpenType fonts, and usually include 1/8, 3/8, 5/8, 7/8, and sometimes 1/3 and 2/3. Arbitrary fractions include anything and everything else, such as 18/256. (See Sample Below and my Blog on "About Well Defined Fractions")

Choosing Glyphs

A glyph is a single representation of a character. Every font has a Unicode character map that links (abstract) character IDs with how to display that character, using the default glyphs. A single character can have multiple glyphs (alternates), and a single glyph can represent multiple characters (ligatures). (See Sample Below)

Open Type in Microsoft Word

Those who use Microsoft Word will note that Word has limited Open Type support and uses. What are generally available, if the font in question has them, are Stylistic Alternates, Contextual Alternates and Standard and Discretionary Ligatures. Thus, the fl ligature, for example, can be accessed in Word (See Example Below). If the Open Type font has fractions that go beyond the normal fractional glyphs, they will also be available in Word documents. Most likely, however, fractions that are real typographic fractions are limited in Word usage.

To access these features in Word, (1) Select your text and go to to Format > Font and select the Advanced tab. (2) For Stylistic Alternates, click on the drop-down menu under "Stylistic Sets" and choose one of the sets. Keep in mind that not all fonts will have 20 stylistic sets. (3) To enable contextual alternates, check the box toward the bottom. Ligatures — If you click on the drop-down beside Ligatures you'll be able to choose from Standard ligatures, Historical and Discretionary, and so forth. (See Sample Below)

To access Open Type glyphs in other text programs, you have to use what is called PUA Unicode-mapping. Unicode has been around for several decades, but it didn't come into the limelight until 2000 when Adobe and Microsoft jointly adopted Unicode for font encoding. Today, Unicode is the default character encoding for nearly all computer technologies. Unicode is a common character set that is supported on the Windows, Apple, and Unix platforms. It assigns a unique number (called a code point) to each character of the world's major languages, plus mathematical symbols, common decorative symbols like checkboxes, diacritical marks, punctuation, and other characters. Unicode supports more than 900,000 code points which means it can handle more than 900,000 characters or glyphs. That's a huge increase from legacy TrueType and PostScript fonts which had only 256 code points.

Consequently, using Unicode, a typist can access characters such as true prime (U 2032), double prime (U 2033) and true quotes. For Windows users, (1) Open the Windows Character Map App; (2) Set the Font to the desired one in the list; (3) At the bottom, check [ ] Advanced View; (4) Set "Group by:" to Unicode Subrange; (5) At the bottom of the list, select "Private Use Characters." You can also use a glyph finder app like "PopChar" (https://ergonis.com/popchar $29.99)

For Mac users, (1) Open the FontBook app; (2) To copy characters, go to Preview / View > Repertoire; (3) Select and copy (CMD + C) the desired character; (4) You can then paste (CMD + V) the character(s) into the text field of your open program (such as Microsoft Word.) Or, you can use an app, like PopChar or Ultra Character Map (https://x04studios. com/ultracharactermap.html $9.99 for Mac)

The point is that Open Type has a myriad range of use and features open to the general and specialized user of open type fonts. Enjoy getting to know and use them in your documents!

(*Much of this article is adapted from the Creative Market blog, https://support. creativemarket.com/hc/en-us/articles/360037478813-Using-Fonts-with-Special-Features-OpenType-#opentype)

InDesign "Character" Window

To access this Window in InDesign go to the "Window" menu, "Type & Tables"
To access any Open Type features, click on the upper right hash marks

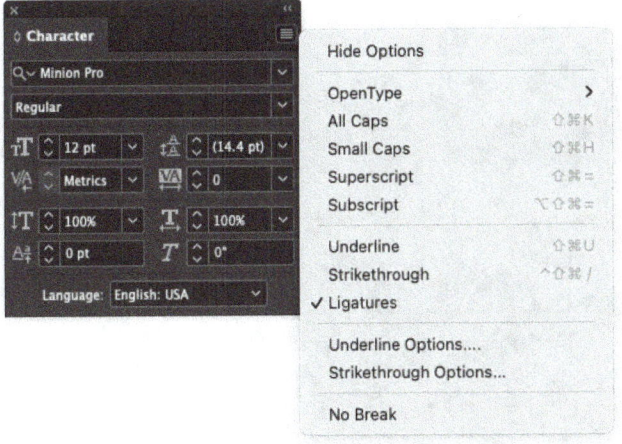

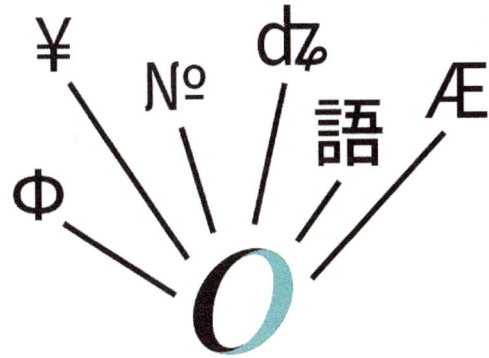

$$AE \rightarrow \text{Æ} \qquad ij \rightarrow \text{ÿ}$$

$$ae \rightarrow \text{œ} \qquad st \rightarrow \text{ſt}$$

$$OE \rightarrow \text{Œ} \qquad ft \rightarrow \text{ft}$$

$$oe \rightarrow \text{œ} \qquad et \rightarrow \text{ẽ}$$

$$ff \rightarrow \text{ff} \qquad fs \rightarrow \text{ß}$$

$$fi \rightarrow \text{fi} \qquad ffi \rightarrow \text{ffi}$$

Book Antiqua Font 18pt.
Fractions in Microsoft Word
¼ ½ ¾ but not 3/16

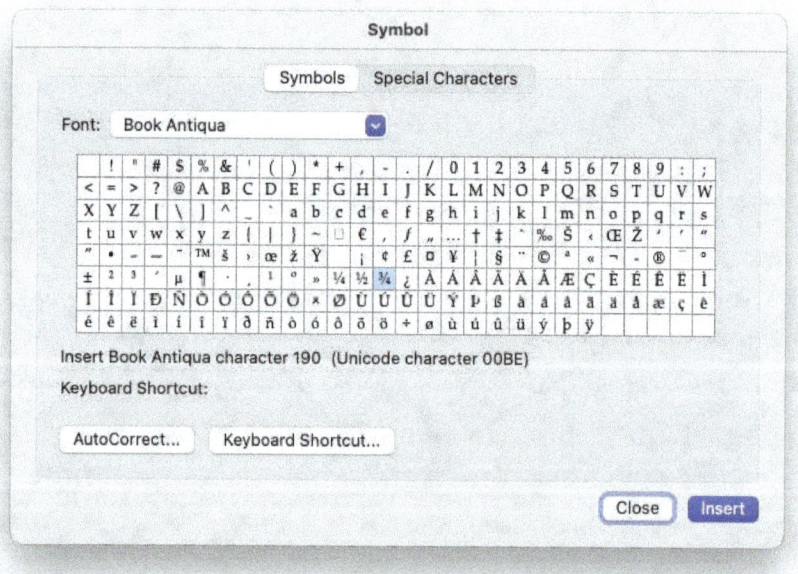

standard

Alegreya Font 36 pt
"st" Discretionary Ligature glyph
Unicode 0073 + 0074

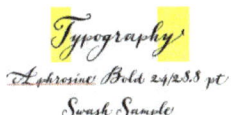

Typography

Aphrosine Bold 24/28.8 pt
Swash Sample

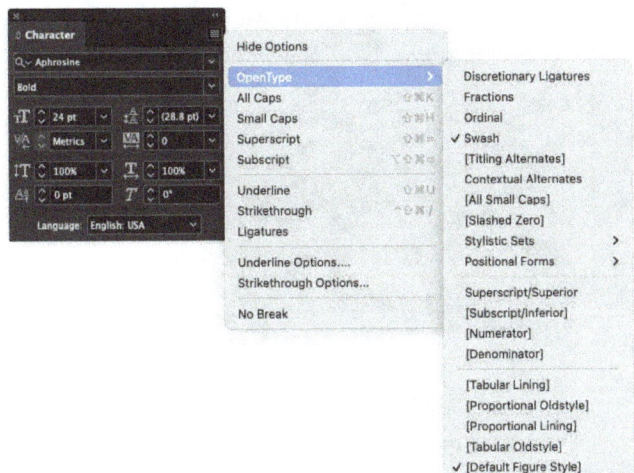

Typography ⁵⁄₁₆

Bilo Medium 36/43.2 pt
Adobe InDesign
ORDINALS & FRACTIONS

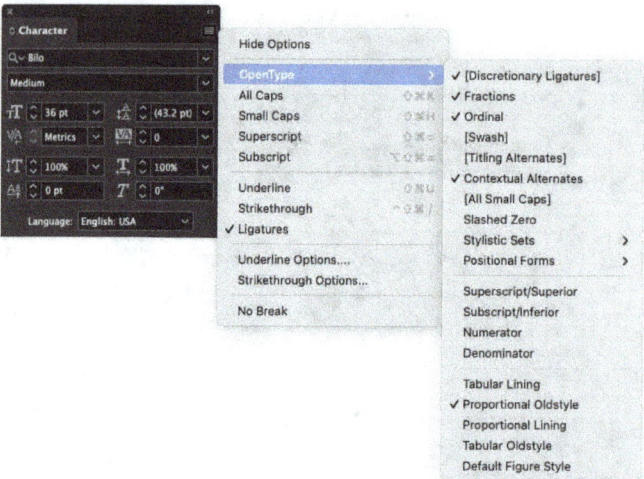

Microsoft Word Advanced Font Menu

To access this Window in Microsoft Word, go to "Font,"
then "Advanced."

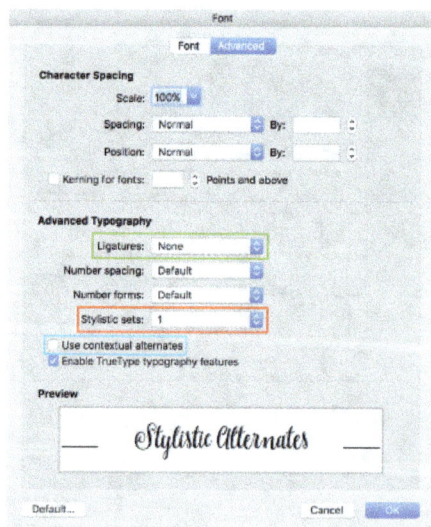

Ultra Character App for Mac

Ultra Character Map lets you access any character or glyph in any font and use it in other apps. It also lets you do side-by-side font comparisons, print font catalogs, view detailed character and font information including the keystroke combinations that produce special or accented characters and much more.

What's In A Name?

The Typographical History of Your Name

"ABCDEFG
HIJKLMNOP
QRSTUV
WXYZ
Now I said my ABCs
What do you think of me?"
(The Alphabet Song)

Do you remember memorizing your ABCs with the "Alphabet Song?" Our entire life has been framed by the alphabet. For those of us in the typography or typesetting business, the alphabet is our bread-and-butter. Those of us who design fonts and tweak layouts and redesign business logos are, may I say, in love with the alphabet and all that it conveys.

But even if you are only slightly interested in history and the alphabet, have you ever wondered where your name came from? Not your surname, which you can find on sites such as *ancestry.com*, but your NAME, that which people casually call you. My name is "Carl," and I have wondered where those letters came from in the history of letter forms and cultural associations.

Alphabet History. The Alphabet is old. Very old. John Coleman Darnell, an Egyptologist from Yale University, in the 1990s made a discovery that rocked the alphabetic world. Looking for Egyptian relics, he discovered two ancient inscriptions at Wadi El-hol in central Egypt, about 30 miles northwest of ancient Thebes.

This ancient road had evidence of inscriptions on the walls of the cliffs lining the roadway. The writings show the alphabet's invention from around

2000 BC. A fascinating study of his report is found in David Sacks, *Letter Perfect: The Marvelous History of Our Alphabet From A to Z*.

The Egyptians wrote in hieroglyphics (called "sacred carvings"), using pictograms for letters. Pictures of familiar objects were used to convey sounds and words. The ancient Semites borrowed from these pictograms, so that, for example, the picture of a "head" was called resh, and since the word began with the sound of an "r," they selected that image for the sound. Thus, "R" is the sketch of a head.

From these backgrounds, the Phoenicians, descendants of people who lived in ancient Canaan, began writing their language in a 22-letter alphabet, sometime before 1000 BC. They had inherited these letters from other tribes before them, but had the skill and knowledge to formally write them down. By 900 BC the Jews and other Near Eastern peoples copied the letters for their own use. The Greeks then followed about 800 BC, adapting the letters for their own use. The chart below shows the Phoenician alphabet and how it relates to our modern alphabet.

Beyond the Phoenicians. The Phoenician alphabet fostered the Greek which fostered the Etruscan, a people who lived in northern Italy. From there, the Roman alphabet and writing were developed. The Phoenician alphabet had 22 letters, while the Greek alphabet had 26. Interestingly, the Hebrews, another Semitic tribe which populated the Canaanite region under the influence of Joshua's campaign (in the Bible in Deuteronomy 31), only khet (ח), qof (ק), resh (ר) and shin (ש) resemble their Phoenician counterparts. The Hebrew writing from right-to-left derives from the Phoenicians.

Modern letter forms have their immediate heritage in Roman inscriptions from around 50–120 AD. The digital version called Trajan, created by Carol Twombly in 1989 for Adobe, reveals some of these Latin forms. In the sixth through tenth centuries, lower case letters (called minuscules) were formed, with modern lettering evolving from the Carolingian scripts.

The Emperor Charlemagne used these letters as an educational standard. The Charlemagne font, created by Carol Twombly again, can be seen in the Latin lettering in the sample above. Italics then came into being in the form of cursive script developed in Rome and Florence.

Researching my name. So, with all this information, and more, I investigated the letter forms that make up my name, CARL. The examples below show that tracing. If you would like more information on tracing your own name, buy a copy of David Sacks, *Letter Perfect: The Marvelous History of Our Alphabet from A to Z*, available at Amazon.com.

Early Font History

ALPHABET	Phoenician	Hebrew	Greek	Latin
A		א	A α	A
B		ב	B β	B
C				C
D		ד	Δ δ	D
E			E ε	E
F			Φ φ	F
G		ג	Γ γ	G
H		ה	H η	H
I			I ι	I
J				J
K		כ	K κ	K
L		ל	Λ λ	L
M		מ	M μ	M
N		נ	N ν	N
O			O o	O
P		פ	Π π	P
Q		ק		Q
R		ר	P ρ	R
S		ס	Σ σ	S
T		ת	T τ	T
U			Y υ	U
V		ו		V
W			Ω ω	W
X				X
Y				Y
Z			Z ζ	Z
Special		ח "kh"	Θ θ "th"	
		צ "ts"	Ξ ξ "x"	
		ע	Ψ ψ "ps"	
		ט "t"	X χ "ch"	
		שׁ "sh"		

The Trajan Font

A B C D E F G H I J
K L M N O P Q
R S T U V W X Y Z
1234567890
{ } i ¢ £ ¥ © ® ƒ ™

Born in 1959 in Concord, CT, Carol Twombly studied at the Rhode Island School of Design and at Stanford University. She was awarded 1st prize in the Morisawa type competition in Japan for the Mirarae typeface in 1984. She joined Adobe in 1988 and designed Adobe's first original display typefaces (Trajan, Charlemagne and Lithos). Fonts: Mirarae (1984), (1989), (1989), (1989), (1990), (1992), Viva (1993), Nueva (1994) and Chaparral (1997).

The inscription on the base of the Trajan column in Rome is an example of classic Roman letterforms, which reached their peak of refinement in the first century A.D. It is believed that the letters were first written with a brush, then carved into the stone. These forms provided the basis for this Adobe Originals typeface designed by Carol Twombly in 1989. Trajan is an elegant typeface well-suited for display work in books, magazines, posters, and billboards.

The Letter C
(Formata Bold, 30 pt)

The letter "C" started unlike any recognizable "C" we would know, except for Egyptian Hieroglyphic or Semitic peoples who said the third letter of the alphabet was a "throwing stick."

Egyptian
"Throwing Stick"

In about 1000 BC the Phoenician and Canaanite peoples gave a linear form to the third place in their alphabet. The sign was called a *gimel*, or "throwing stick" or "boomerang."

Phoenician
"gimel"

The Greeks around 800 BC kept the letter at number three in the alphabet, reversed the letter, with the sound of "g," but altered the name to *gamma*. The ancient Hebrew/Semitic letter is ℷ read right-to-left, and is used in the Massoretic text of the Old Testament of the Bible.

Greek
"gamma"

The straight line gamma morphed to a crescent gamma around 675 BC, and then the Etruscans of northern Italy around 500 BC adopted the crescent shape. It still possessed the hard "g" sound.

Etruscan C

The Romans borrowed from the Etruscans and rounded the letter even more so. Originally, the sound was either a hard "g" or a "k" sound. Eventually, a C plus a bar became the "G" or "G" we know.

Roman C

Modern renderings of "C" can be found in typography using programs like Fontographer, or Extensis' FontLab. The most modern formulation from Adobe FireFly is a sans-serif bold "C" infused through generative AI (artificial intelligence) with an ancient typographical design.

Fontographer C   FireFly C

The Letter A
(Formata Bold, 30 pt)

Ox Head

The letter "A" started out looking like an ox head, as found by lime-stone carved inscriptions at Wadi el-Hol in 1992, inscribed we believe by mercenary soldiers around 1800 BC. We are not sure why "A" is first, but some say it symbolizes the creative energy of God that initiated creation. The ancient Hebrew/Semitic letter is א read right-to-left, and is used in the Massoretic text of the Old Testament of the Bible.

Phoenician A

The choice of an ox to represent the "A" sound would have been normal for the Phoenicians, since the ox was a main source of heavy work and food. The "V" with a slash distinguished the horns from the face, calling the letter *alif*. About 800 BC the letter as seen by the Greeks is now slanted.

Greek "alpha"   **Later Greek**

The Greeks transcribed the first letter of the alphabet looking more like our "K" than an "A." They also renamed the letter *alpha*. In 740 BC the letter was turned on its side because of reading left-to-right. Evidence from 720 BC shows the letter is now upright.

Etruscan A   **Roman A**

The Romans learn from the Etruscan traders of northern Italy. The name of the first letter was changed to "ah." The Roman capital letters have endured through time and have been the standard for proportion and dignity, according to Allan Haley.

Small a   **Handwritten small a**

In the fourth century small "a" was given a circular shape with a projection, forming the parent of the handwritten and printed small "a."

Fontographer A   **FireFly A**

Modern renderings of "A" can be found in typography using programs like Fontographer, or Extensis' FontLab. The most modern formulation from Adobe FireFly is a sans-serif bold "A" infused through generative AI (artificial intelligence) with an ancient typographical design.

The Letter R

(Formata Bold, 30 pt)

R = Head

The Semitic letter "R" probably started from an Egyptian hieroglyph of a human head in profile about 1800 BC. It is the 20th letter in our alphabet. It is *resh* and means "head."

Phoenician R
"resh"

The Phoenician "R" for resh still shows a head profile, but turned the opposite way because of the right-to-left Semitic reading of the time.

Greek R
"rho"

The Greek letter "R" for *rho* from about 750 BC dulicated the Phoenician letter for shape, sound and alphabetic place. They turned the letter around for left-to-right reading and added a tail. The ancient Hebrew/Semitic letter is ר read right-to-left, still number 20 in the Hebrew alphabet, and is used in the Massoretic text of the Old Testament of the Bible. It still means "head."

Roman R

The Romans took a signal from the Greeks, adding a tail to the "R" form to distinguish it from their "P."

Medieval
small r

Handwritten
small r

In medieval times the small "r" was made with a stroke to connect it to succeeding letters. David Sacks notes that "this pleasant little shape was then copied by the humanist handwriting school of Italy in the early 1400s. From there, the 'r' was taken up by early printers in Italy, who copied humanist letter shapes in designing lowercase letters of type (around 1470)."

Fontographer R

FireFly R

Modern renderings of "R" can be found in typography using programs like Fontographer, or Extensis' FontLab. The most modern formulation from Adobe FireFly is a sans-serif bold "R" infused through generative AI (artificial intelligence) with an ancient typographical design.

The Letter L
(Formata Bold, 30 pt)

The letter "L" is the 12th letter of the alphabet, found on the earliest inscriptions in Wadi el-Hol about 1800 BC.

L = Ox Goad

The Phoenician "L" for *lamed* named the "ox goad," about 800 BC. The lamed is pointing backward because of right-to-left writing and indicates a shepherd's hook or goad on the end.

**Phoenician L
"lamed"**

The Greek letter "L" for *lambda* from about 725 BC pointing backward toward the preceding letter. The ancient Hebrew/Semitic letter is ל read right-to-left, and is used in the Massoretic text of the Old Testament of the Bible.

**Greek L
"lambda"**

The Roman "L" early on imitated the Etruscan alphabet letter, which was copied into the Roman alphabet in 600 BC. The beautiful "L" of the 100s AD, which became a standard for all succeeding serif "L's."

Roman L

In late Roman times, the small handwritten "l" was developed from the capital letter with rounded lines. As the Italian humanist period approached, the flowing humanist shapes live on in the Garamond type sample based on designs of the 1500s.

**Handwritten
small l**

**Humanist
small l**

Modern renderings of "L" can be found in typography using programs like Fontographer, or Extensis' FontLab. The most modern formulation from Adobe FireFly is a sans-serif bold "L" infused through generative AI (artificial intelligence) with an ancient typographical design.

**Fontographer L
Garamond Bold**

FireFly L

Ancient Alphabets

More Alphabetic History

*"Symbols resembling hieroglyphs had been used by artisans
in the region since 4000 BC, but with no ascertainable linguistic content.
The first hieroglyphs were used for making inscriptions on buildings and tombs."
(Google Fonts on Noto Sans Egyptian Hieroglyphs)*

Ancient alphabets. How did our alphabet come to exist? Much of what we know about the alphabet comes from Middle Eastern and Egyptian sources. In my previous chapter ("What's In A Name?"), I investigated the creation of the alphabet and how our modern letters were formed. Again, I refer the interested reader and researcher to the excellent work by David Sacks, *Letter Perfect: The Marvelous History of Our Alphabet from A to Z*, available at Amazon.com. This particular chapter offers readers and historical users the opportunity to see and download several ancient alphabetic fonts that history has uncovered.

It should be noted that in the computer world, Google fonts has produced several ancient fonts, only in Unicode offerings. They are Noto Sans Cuneiform, Noto Sans Egyptian Hieroglyphs, Noto Sans Ugaritic, Noto Sans Old Persian and Noto Sans Imperial Aramaic. These are extensive fonts with hundreds or even thousands of characters in Unicode format. What that means is that finding a particular pictogram or etching (what ancient fonts look like) for a particular letter is next to impossible, unless one knows the exact letter font coding. They are also open source fonts, available for use and reconstitution.

Using a reliable historical source, we can match letters or numbers to font glyphs. Consequently, what CARE Typography has been able to do is to recreate some of these ancient fonts that match the alphabet's capital lettering. Thus, in the Noto Sans font for Egyptian Hieroglyphs when you type the letter "A" you get back "A," not the Egyptian Hieroglyph for "A." The same holds true for the other Noto Sans fonts. We were able to reformulate some of the ancient fonts so that "A," for instance, gives you the correct ancient letter or pictogram. Note the diagrams below.

EgyptHiero. This is the reconstituted Noto Sans Egyptian Hieroglyph only for the capital letters of our alphabet. A bit of history here. Egyptian hieroglyphics were used for writing the Egyptian language from about 3000 BC until 400 AD. Symbols resembling hieroglyphs had been used by artisans in the region since 4000 BC, but with no ascertainable linguistic content. The first hieroglyphs were used for making inscriptions on buildings and tombs. Later they came to be used to decorate jewelry, record events on papyrus and to put a royal or divine signature, called a *cartouche* on an item. The Egyptian hieroglyphic system of writing consisted of both phonetic symbols and pictographs. There were about 30 symbols representing single consonants.

UgariticCuneform. This is the reconstituted Noto Sans Ugaritic font only for the capital letters of our alphabet. Ugaritic is a historical Middle Eastern abjad, written left-to-right. Was used in today's Syria in 1500-1300 BC for the Ugaritic language, and also for Hurrian. Has 30 letters that visually resemble cuneiform. The Ugaritic script was used from about 1500-1300 BC to write the Ugaritic language, spoken in modern-day Syria. It was also occasionally used for writing documents in the Hurrian language. Visually, the script resembled Cuneiform, with each letter written as one of a combination of short, linear wedges.

OldPersianA. This is the reconstituted Noto Sans Old Persian font, again only for the capital letters of our alphabet. Old Persian cuneiform was the main script for writing the Old Persian language from 525-330 BC. Visually it resembles Sumero-Akkadian cuneiform; most of the letters are arrangements of between two and five horizontal, vertical or angle-shaped wedges. However, there appears to be no derivational relationship between the sound-to-symbol mapping of individual letters in the two scripts, nor has any other script been found which links the forms of the scripts. For this reason, Old Persian cuneiform is generally believed to have been an independent invention.

These particular crafted fonts can be ordered *for free* from CARE Typography at cshanktype@gmail.com.

Ancient Fonts Alphabets

UgariticCuneform

A	⊷
B	ℼ
C	⁂
D	Ⅲ
E	
F	⊥
G	❘
H	❘
I	⊫
J	◁
K	▷
L	Ⅲ
M	⅂
N	⊷
O	❮
P	⊨
Q	⊰
R	⇉
S	ᛉ
T	⊢
U	Ⅲ
V	⋤
W	⊳
X	◁Ⅴ
Y	⅋
Z	❘

UgariticCuneform is a working adaptation of the Noto Sans Ugaritic Google Font. The Google font is practically unusable being a Unicode Font.

Ugaritic is a historical Middle Eastern *abjad*, written left-to-right. Was used in today's Syria in 1500-1300 BC for the Ugaritic language, and also for Hurrian. Has 30 letters that visually resemble cuneiform.

The Ugaritic script was used from about 1500-1300 BC to write the Ugaritic language, spoken in modern-day Syria. It was also occasionally used for writing documents in the Hurrian language. Visually, the script resembled Cuneiform, with each letter written as one of a combination of short, linear wedges. However, the forms of the letters appear to have been freely invented; derivational relationships with other cuneiform letters have not been established. The script remained relatively stable in form throughout its use, with no significant changes.

Ugaritic was generally written from left to right with a vertical slash dividing words. Rarely, it was also written from right to left. There were thirty letters used, all representing consonants. Three of these, called aleph, represented a glottal stop, each with a different vowel associated with it. The vowels [a], [i] and [u] were represented in this way. The letter representing [j] was also sometimes used as a vowel. Letters were ordered into one of two orders. The "Northern Semitic order" more closely resembles the order of Hebrew and Greek letters, and the "Southern Semitic order" more closely resembles that of South Arabian and Ge'ez letters.

Letters were aligned to a midline. No punctuation was used apart from the inter-word slash. (Courtesy fonts.google.com & scriptsource.org)

CARE Typography carefully recreated the slashes for the requisite lettering, giving access to the capital letters of the alphabet for use.

Ancient Fonts Alphabets

Old PersianA

A	𐎠
B	𐎲
C	𐎣
D	𐎭
E	𐎡
F	𐎳
G	𐎥
H	𐏃
I	𐎡
J	𐎩
K	𐎣
L	𐎾
M	𐎶
N	𐎴
O	𐎢
P	𐎱
Q	𐎤
R	𐎼
S	𐎿
T	𐎫
U	𐎢
V	𐎺
W	𐎺
X	𐎧
Y	𐎹
Z	𐎰

OldPersianA is a working adaptation of the Noto Sans Old Persian Google Font. The Google font is practically unusable being a Unicode Font.

Noto Sans Old Persian is an unmodulated ("sans serif") design for texts in the historical Middle Eastern Old Persian script. The original Noto Sans Old Persian contains 55 glyphs, and supports 54 characters from the Unicode block Old Persian.

Old Persian cuneiform was the main script for writing the Old Persian language from 525-330 BC. Visually it resembles Sumero-Akkadian cuneiform; most of the letters are arrangements of between two and five horizontal, vertical or angle-shaped wedges. However, there appears to be no derivational relationship between the sound-to-symbol mapping of individual letters in the two scripts, nor has any other script been found which links the forms of the scripts. For this reason, Old Persian cuneiform is generally believed to have been an independent invention.

Old Persian was written from left to right and encoded three vowel ([a/a:], [i/i:] and [u/u:]) and twenty-two consonant sounds using three vowel and thirty-three consonant letters. Vowel length was generally not indicated; the exception to this was a long [a:] vowel. All vowels except for short [a] were written, so the script was essentially an alphabet, with some syllabic properties. The twenty-two consonant signs were of two types. For thirteen consonant sounds, the following vowel sound was represented by the following vowel sign (or lack thereof). These consonants contained an inherent short 'a' vowel; when this vowel was missing its absence was not indicated in any way. So p – [p] or [pa]. When the letter was followed by an a letter, it indicated a long [a:] vowel: p+a – [pa:] but p+i – [pi] or [pi:] and p+u – [pu] or [pu:]. The remaining nine consonant sounds each had a different shape depending on the quality of the following vowel. Of these, only 'd' and 'm' had three different forms to represent [-a/a:/Ø], [-i/i:] and [-u/u:]. The remaining seven letters only had a two-way distinction, either to distinguish [-u/u:] from [-a/a:/i/i:], or because only two of the three vowels were ever used after that particular consonant. For those nine signs whose shape already implies the following vowel, the vowel was still written as a separate letter. So the sound [di/i:] was written with two letters di+i. This enabled diphthongs following one of these nine consonants to be easily expressed; da+i represented [dai]. Diphthongs following one of the other thirteen consonants were a little more ambiguous; the letters p+i could represent either [pi/i:] or [pai] because of the possible inherent 'a' vowel.

Some letters were subject to further orthographic rules; n and (before stops) m were not written at the end of a syllable, and h was not written before u or m. The vowel i was generally not written after h. In addition to the thirty-six phonetic letters, seven ideograms were used to represent common words or divine names, and there was a set of base numbers representing 1, 2, 10, 20, 100. These were added cumulatively with the biggest numbers to the left to represent other numbers, for example 5–2+2+1, 13–10+2+1, 60–20+20+20 etc. (Courtesy fonts.google.com & scriptsource.org)

CARE Typography carefully recreated the slashes for the requisite lettering, giving access to the capital letters of the alphabet for use.

Ancient Fonts Alphabets

EgyptHiero

A	
B	
C	
D	
E	
F	
G	
H	
I	
J	
K	
L	
M	
N	
O	
P	
Q	
R	
S	
T	
U	
V	
W	
X	
Y	
Z	

EgyptHiero is a working adaptation of the Noto Sans Egyptian Hieroglyphics Google Font. The Google font is practically unusable being a Unicode Font.

Noto Sans Egyptian Hieroglyphs is an unmodulated ("sans serif") design for texts in the historical African Egyptian hieroglyphs script. Noto Sans Egyptian Hieroglyphs contains 1,079 glyphs, and supports 1,078 characters from the Unicode block Egyptian Hieroglyphs.

Egyptian hieroglyphics were used for writing the Egyptian language from about 3000 BC until 400 AD. Symbols resembling hieroglyphs had been used by artisans in the region since 4000 BC, but with no ascertainable linguistic content. The first hieroglyphs were used for making inscriptions on buildings and tombs. Later they came to be used to decorate jewelry, record events on papyrus and to put a royal or divine signature, called a *cartouche* on an item.

The Egyptian hieroglyphic system of writing consisted of both phonetic symbols and pictographs. There were about 30 symbols representing single consonants, plus about 130 bilateral and trilateral symbols which represented two or three consonants. For example, the heart-with-trachea symbol represented the consonants n + f + r, pronounced nefer. Some symbols were used as phonetic complements, which reinforced the final consonant in a bi- or trilateral symbol. Vowels were not written. Pictograms were symbols which visually resembled the item or concept they represented. In total there were an estimated 7000 pictograms, but these were not all in use at the same time. Some symbols could be used either as a pictogram or as a phonetic symbol. For example, a rectangular spiral represented both the sound [pr], and the concept of a house. Combined with the fact that vowels were not written, this resulted in some symbols or combinations of symbols having multiple possible meanings. To indicate which meaning was intended, a third class of symbol, called *determinatives*, was used. Often, a small vertical stroke underneath the symbol was used to indicate that the object/concept - rather than the phonetic - interpretation was intended. Another example of a determinative was a pictogram of a pair of legs to indicate that the preceding symbol was a verb of movement.

Egyptian hieroglyphic writing did not use any punctuation or word spacing. Symbols were arranged either in vertical columns or horizontal rows, and could be read from right to left or from left to right. In order to demonstrate in which direction the text had been written, the scribe would orientate any animate pictograms (that is, symbols in the shape of a human or animal) to face in the intended direction of reading. (Courtesy fonts.google.com & scriptsource.org)

CARE Typography carefully used the pictograms in the original Unicode font for the requisite lettering, giving access to the capital letters of the alphabet for use.

Ancient Fonts Alphabets

Demotic Script

Upper		Lower		Num/Sym	
A	ꜣ	a	?	1	˩
B		b		2	\\
C		c		3	ʒ
D		d		4	⁗
E		e	‖	5	ʒ
F		f		6	˥
G		g		7	˥
H		h	ꓶ	8	ʒ
I		i	꜓	9	˥
J		j		0	
K		k		!	ꓵ
L		l		@	˧
M		m		#	ꓭ
N		n		%	ꓮ
O		o	ꓤ		
P		p			
Q		q			
R		r			
S		s			
T		t			
U		u			
V		v			
W		w			
X		x			
Y		y			
Z		z			

The Egyptian Demotic script was used from about 600 BC to about 400 AD for writing the Egyptian language. Demotic writing descended from Egyptian Hieratic writing, the manuscript writing system which was used alongside Hieroglyphics, and it was later used in place of both of these scripts. The development of the Demotic script is generally divided into three periods, Early, Middle (Ptolemaic) and Late (Roman). Demotic was mostly written on papyrus, embalming fabric and other soft surfaces, but was sometimes also inscribed in stone, the most famous example being the middle section of the Rosetta Stone. Initially the script was used primarily in an administrative context; later it came to be used for literary and religious texts also. It was gradually supplanted by the Coptic alphabet from 300 AD onwards.

Egyptian Demotic was a cursive script, written from right to left. It was similar in form to hieroglyphic and hieratic writing, in that it used a combination of logographic and phonetic signs. It reproduced many of the same shapes of the pictographs of the earlier scripts, in a more cursive form which no longer necessarily resembled the concepts/objects they represented. New words for which there was no pre-existing sign were spelled using phonetic symbols. (Courtesy scriptsource.org)

Demotic Script has been offered by Egyptology Lessons as seen on YouTube.

Ancient Fonts Alphabets

a	ည	1	۱
b	ໄ	2	៱
c	✔	3	z
d	♩	4	៥
e	‿	5	ៀ
f	✔	6	♬
g	ၮ	7	♔
h	⅏		
i	⊦		
j	↑		
k	∧		
l	⤸		
m	ℨ		
n	‑		
o	↑		
p	⅏		
q	⅊		
r	◅		
s	⅃		
t	∠		
u	♙		
v	⤳		
w	⅃		
x	⊏		
y	⅄		
z	⇢		

Hieratic script, ancient Egyptian cursive writing, used from the 1st dynasty (c. 2925–c. 2775 BC) until about 200 BC. Derived from the earlier, pictorial hieroglyphic writing used in carved or painted inscriptions, hieratic script was generally written in ink with a reed pen on papyrus; its cursive form was more suited to such a medium than were the formal hieroglyphs. It was originally written vertically and later horizontally from right to left.

The Hieratic script was invented and developed more or less at the same time as the hieroglyphic script and was used in parallel with it for everyday purposes such as keeping records and accounts and writing letters. It was used until the 26th Dynasty, though by that time, it was only used for religious texts, while the Demotic script was used for most other purposes.

Its notable features included a simplified and abbreviated form of the hieroglyphic script in which the people, animals and object depicted are no longer easily recognizable. It was structurally the same as the hieroglyphic script Written almost exclusively from right to left in horizontal lines and mainly in ink on papyrus. It was written in a number of different styles such as "business hand" and the more elaborate "book hand."

There were a number of regional variations, one of which, a northern version, developed into the Demotic script by the 25th Dynasty. (Courtesy britannica.com and omniglot.com)

Hieratic Script has been offered by Egyptology Lessons as seen on YouTube.

Ancient Fonts Extended

ALPHABET	Ugaritic Cuneiform	Old Persian	HieraticScript[1]	Demotic Script[2]	Egyptian Hieroglyphs	Phoenician	Hebrew	Greek
A								A α
B								B β
C								
D								Δ δ
E								E ε
F								Φ φ
G								Γ γ
H								H η
I								I ι
J								
K								K κ
L								Λ λ
M								M μ
N								N ν
O								O ο
P								Π π
Q								
R								P ρ
S								Σ σ
T								T τ
U								Y υ
V								
W								Ω ω
X								Ξ ξ "x"
Y								
Z								Z ζ

		Θ θ "th"
		Ψ ψ "ps"
	"kh"	X χ "ch"
	"ts"	
	"t"	
	"sh"	

SPECIAL DEMOTIC

1 =	! = n	3 =
2 =	# =	4 =
3 =	$ =	5 =
4 =	% =	6 =
5 =	@ =	7 =
6 =	1 =	8 =
7 =	2 =	9 =

(1) HIERATIC SCRIPT BY EGYPTOLOGYLESSONS.
(2) DEMOTIC SCRIPT FONT BY EGYPTOLOGYLESSONS.
SEE HTTPS://EN.WIKIPEDIA.ORG/WIKI/HIERATIC FOR MORE
INFORMATION. ALSO SEE HIS YOUTUBE POST.

Kern, Kern, Kern

Bringing Letters Together

"The process of improving appearance and
legibility by adjusting the white space between
certain paired characters."
(*Type Terminology,* Altsys Corporation)

T he importance of *kerning.* Do you recall the song, "Turn, Turn, Turn" written by Pete Seeger in 1959 and sung by The Byrds? Perhaps not, depending on your age and music likes and dislikes, but another "song" for typographers is "Kern, Kern, Kern," initially written by Gene Gable in *Publish* magazine in December 1993. He advances the cause of kerning type for a smooth and even look, especially at very large sizes of font use in advertising and posters.

First things first, however. Perhaps you know there is an invisible space between characters, an invisible box. In original days of printing presses, typographers would look at this space and, if too much space occurred between letters, they would cut notches in wooden blocks to help letters fit together more evenly and aesthetically. As typesetting advanced into phototypesetting, the space around each character would be altered by moving a prism along a track. From this practice, we get tracking of type.

Sometimes the difference between *kerning* and *tracking* of type is not known. *Tracking* involves the spacing between all characters in a given section of text or headline. Tracking affects the overall "color" or character density within a given block of text. Tracking is also know as "letterspacing," and refers to the visual "looseness" or "tightness" of text in a block.

Kerning, on the other hand, refers to pairs of letters that are supposed to fit together in a pleasing way. Awkward looking gaps between letters, at whatever point size, are to be dealt with by "kerning" letters. In the old days of printing presses, typographers would fix this problem by cutting notches in the wooden blocks to help the letters fit closer together in a more visually pleasing way.

Kerning is a subjective art. Not enough, perhaps, is said about this aspect of pairs of letters and how they look to observers. How you "see" something has to be taken into account in talking about kerning. Does this look like enough space? Does it look like too much? Are the letters too tight or too loose?

You need both *readability* and *legibility*, with legibility referring to the finer details of typography. Readability refers to a reader being able to absorb the body of your text. You need to watch out for certain letter combinations, like the slanted letters, A, K, V, W, Y, letters with arms or cross strokes: F, L, T, and letter combinations: W or V + A (any order); T or F + a lowercase vowel or a period or comma. The Adriatic font below shows how such combinations can look bad, even with a decent formed font design.

Lower case letters need special attention, as well, with two straight letters needing the most space, a straight and a round letter needing less space and two round letters even less space. While the letters viewed on their own may look evenly spaced, it is the letter combinations that tell if proper kerning has taken place. Point sizes of letters need special attention, with larger sizes in posters, or ads, or logos needing manual kerning.

Kerning mistakes will be glaring while working with large, highly visible letters. Special attention needs to be given to text that is tightly spaced, especially in combinations like "r" plus "n," where they may indeed run together.

Use kerning strategically. While most major typographers offer from a minimum of 400 pairs to over 1,000 pairs, there are actually over 30,000 possible letter combinations that could concern the typographer. Expert type has been set by people with outstanding kerning skills and meticulous care.

Thus, Sumner Stone from Adobe suggests that some typographers overdo tightness. Use H and O as reference characters, both a flat and a curved edge. Best yet, use a well-designed typeface, such as the Arno Pro face shown in the example below. Take the font x-height into account for readability, with the knowledge that typefaces with large x-heights are generally more readable at smaller sizes. get creative with manual kerning in posters and logos. Take FedEx, for instance, with negative space between the letters forming the well-known arrow of the company.

Some suggestions for proper kerning would be:

(1) Get a good layout program like Adobe InDesign for special type projects use. Microsoft Word simply does not cut it here.

(2) Use commercially produced fonts made by reputable typographic companies, like Adobe.

(3) Break down your work, especially larger pieces, like posters, into two letter pairs to spot where adjustments need to be made.

(4) Get outside input and comment on your type designs and the use. See what others see.

(5) Turn your work upside down and note the spaces between the letters for a different, maybe more revealing look.

(6) Print your work out in different sizes and adjust kerning where needed.

(7) Be careful of capital letters followed by punctuation or small letters, especially with a serif font.

(8) Practice kerning using an online tool such as Kern Type (https://type.method.ac)

Adobe writers note —"Practice and exposure are the key ingredients to fine-tuning your kerning expertise. Now that you have these tips and tricks in your back pocket, it's time for you to put your kerning know-how into practice."

(https://www.adobe.com/creativecloud/design/discover/kerning.html—ContributorsMadeline DeCotes, Nick Escobar, Robin Casey)

Basic Kerning Pairs

Av	Tw	Wo
Aw	Ty	Wr
Ay	T.	Wu
F.	Va	Wy
P.	Ve	W.
Ta	Vo	Ya
Te	Vu	Ye
To	V.	Yo
Tr	Wa	Yu
Tu	We	Y.

Adobe Arno Pro Font
30 pt

Basic Kerning Pairs

Av	Tw	Wo
Aw	Ty	Wr
Ay	T.	Wu
F.	Va	Wy
P.	Ve	W.
Ta	Vo	Ya
Te	Vu	Ye
To	V.	Yo
Tr	Wa	Yu
Tu	We	Y.

Adobe Garamond Pro Font
30 pt

Basic Kerning Pairs

Av	Tw	Wo
Aw	Ty	Wr
Ay	T.	Wu
F.	Va	Wy
P.	Ve	W.
Ta	Vo	Ya
Te	Vu	Ye
To	V.	Yo
Tr	Wa	Yu
Tu	We	Y.

Adriatic Font
30 pt

Poor Kerning!

Adjusted Kerning Pairs

Av	Tw	Wo
Aw	Ty	Wr
Ay	T.	Wu
F.	Va	Wy
P.	Ve	W.
Ta	Vo	Ya
Te	Vu	Ye
To	V.	Yo
Tr	Wa	Yu
Tu	We	Y.

Adriatic Font
30 pt

(Kerning manually adjusted in InDesign from -75 to -125)

Headline
Avalon

Adriatic font used here has very poor kerning,
though it claims kerning sets have been applied.
Note the wide space between the "H" and "e" and
"A" and "v." The font was created by NovelFonts
Corp. in 1994.

Headline

Avalon

Arno Pro font used here has excellent kerning.
Note the kerned space between the "H" and "e"
and "A" and "v."
The font was meticulously created by
Robert Slimbach from Adobe.

Kerning Examples

Headline Avalon	Courier Font Monospaced Font No kerning; equidistant letters
Headline Avalon	American Typewriter Font Better kerning
Headline Avalon	Times New Roman Acceptable kerning
HEADLINE AVALON	Sava Pro font All caps Better kerning
Headline Avalon	Adobe Garamond Pro Expert kerning

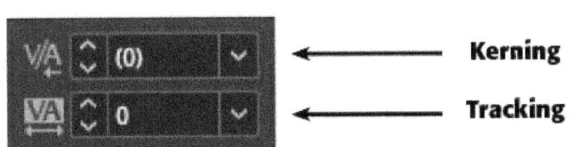

Kerning

Tracking

Adobe InDesign 2024

Copyright Do's & Don't's

The Copyright Law

"The Congress shall have Power . . . to promote
the Progress of Science and useful Arts,
by securing for limited Times to Authors and Inventors
the exclusive Right to their respective Writings and Discoveries."
(*U.S. Constitution*, Article I, Section 8)

Lawyer Sara Hawkins notes that copyright laws are here to encourage the right of creation to authors, rather than to simply deny its use by other people.[1] However, there is a delicate balance to be struck between the creator's rights and the public interest. How do we keep the rights of authors and yet let others use their work?

Copyrights are granted to protect original works of authors, whether it be in literary, written, dramatic, artistic, musical or certain other types of works. Copyrights attach to something once it is created, by a snap of the camera, or the pen of an author, or the sound bites of a musical group. You do not have to file special paperwork for copyright rights, as is the case for trademarks and patents.

Thus, by applying the copyright symbol (©) I have printed and published a number of books and typographic articles and fonts without any special paperwork from the government. The copyright owner can (1) reproduce the copyrighted work; (2) display and publish it publicly; and (3) prepare derivative works based on the copyrighted work.

Copyrights do not apply to works in the public domain, words, names, slogans or short phrases (those may have protection in trademark law), blank forms, works that are not original, and government works. Ideas, procedures, processes, systems, method of operation, concepts, principles or discoveries are not copyrightable.

Thus, the ALPHABET, for example, is not copyrightable. In typography, consequently, you will find "look alikes" of well-crafted typefaces and fonts. Taking photos of copyrighted public access works are allowed. "The copyright in an architectural work that has been constructed does not include the right to prevent the making, distributing, or public display of pictures, paintings, photographs, or other pictorial representations of the work, if the building in which the work is embodied is located in or ordinarily visible from a public place."(Section 120a)

In other words, pictorial representations are permitted of copyrighted works, if the work is located in a public place where everyone and anyone can see it. I have a photo of a bronze statue of Ben Franklin and the printing press, which is located on the grounds of the Masonic Village in Elizabethtown, PA. (See Enclosed photo below) That photo is allowed under copyright laws.

Copyrights are long-lasting. "Copyright in a work created on or after January 1, 1978, subsists from its creation and, except as provided by the following subsections, endures for a term consisting of the life of the author and 70 years after the author's death." (Section 302a) Also, "In the case of an anonymous work, a pseudonymous work, or a work made for hire, the copyright endures for a term of 95 years from the year of its first publication, or a term of 120 years from the year of its creation, whichever expires first." Copying of a work includes printing, photocopying and similar methods of mechanical duplication. It is not permissible to reproduce copyrighted materials without the written authorization of the copyright holder unless it qualifies under the copyright law's doctrine of "fair use."

How do I then legally use a copyrighted work? There are two ways currently available — Get written permission from the creator for its use, or use it perhaps under what is called the "Fair Use" doctrine. Sara Hawkins again says, "The purpose of the Fair Use Doctrine is to allow for limited and reasonable uses as long as the use does not interfere with owners' rights or impede their right to do with the work as they wish."[2]

Fair Use is found in USC Section 107 of the Copyright Laws, and depends on four factors —

(1) *The purpose of use of the copyrighted material.* Fair use of

copyrighted works, as stated in U.S. copyright law, "for purposes such as criticism, comment, news reporting, teaching (including multiple copies for classroom use), scholarship, or research, is not an infringement of copyright." If you are doing a research paper, for instance, you are allowed to quote a copyrighted source, for comment or critique without permission from the original copyright holder. The rules of etiquette require usually footnoting such use. Also, this does not mean, however, that all nonprofit education and noncommercial uses are fair, and that all commercial uses are not fair. Instead, courts will balance the purpose and character of the use against the other three factors below.

(2) *The second test in "Fair Use" cases concerns the nature of the copyrighted work.* Using a more creative or imaginative work (novel, music, movie) would probably not support a Fair Use claim, than a use of a more technical article or a news item. Also, "transformative" uses that adapt the work to something that is decidedly new, with a further purpose or different character, and do not substitute for the original use of the work, can fall under the Fair Use doctrine.

(3) *The third test is the amount and substantiality of the portion used* in relation to the copyrighted work as a whole. If the amount borrowed or used is relatively small in relation to the whole work, this favors a Fair Use finding by the courts. But if the portion used is at the "heart" of a work, this factor will likely weigh against a finding of fair use, even if that portion was otherwise a very small amount.

(4) The fourth test for Fair Use is the *effect of the use upon the potential market for or value of the copyrighted work.* So, as Matthew Goings notes — "An unofficial Seinfeld trivia game would not be not fair use because it could or would affect an official game even though none existed."[3]

He says that "courts evaluate fair use claims on a case-by-case basis, and the outcome of any given case depends on a fact-specific inquiry. This means that there is no formula to ensure that a predetermined percentage or amount of a work—or specific number of words, lines, pages, copies—may be used without permission."[4]

What about AI generated materials and copyright laws? Talk about a thorny issue. Right now, in the courts, there are lawsuits pending against big time AI players such as GitHub and Microsoft and Open AI seeking to see whether or not AI created materials are subject to copyright violations and piracy on a level not seen since the Napster violations in the 1990s.

Getty Images have filed a suit against Stable Diffusion, an AI art developing tool, claiming that its images are too close to the real thing and thus violate copyright laws. This is far from "Fair Use" standards. The Clarkson Law Firm has two class action suits against OpenAI and Google claiming that AI "stole" copyrighted materials from their creators.[5]

Moreover, the U.S. Copyright office has ruled that AI cannot be considered an "author," since only a person can be an author. At present, this is an open-ended issue, and the courts and Congress will have to argue it out. Suffice it to say at this juncture, that using AI to re-create an illustration or an entire book may involve copyright breaches. Be careful in using the technology to bypass coded laws.

What does all of this mean for the typographer or printer or publisher? I would suggest several avenues of using copyrighted materials.

(1) *Seek permission for its use.* This is always the best and most honorable course of action. You may have to contact the publisher, who then in turn may contact the writer. I did this for a study guide I wrote on a book from Oxford Press in England on the life and work of Jonathan Edwards, the great early American theologian in New England.

While it was only a study guide with excerpts on which to comment, and for church study and use exclusively, the Press required a contractural engagement open for one year, with a limited number of copies that could be printed and made available, even for religious study and use. It would have cost me $500 for twelve copies. I declined and went another route with some of the material.

(2) *Use legitimate free sources for photos and images.* I use dreamstime. com in their free portfolios for the background photos and images for a number of book covers I have crafted. There are other legitimate sources in iStock, for instance. Licensing uses and rules apply to most of these freebies. And give credit for where credit is due, even for the freebies.

(3) *Use your own work and photos.* I know this requires substantial time

and effort, but it is usually the right thing to do. I put together a historical calendar of the Lancaster PA area using photos I personally took. (The Calendars are on sale through CARE Typography.)

(4) *Use the old "buyer beware" adage here.* Are you willing to risk your site being taken down, or getting a cease and desist letter, a bill or actually being sued through the Digital Millennium Copyright Act (DMCA), which can be very, very costly. People actually make a living on book royalties and selling or licensing their work. Poaching their work for pleasure or profit is unacceptable.

1.   Sara Hawkins, *Copyright Fair Use and How It Works for Online Images*, https://www.socialmediaexaminer.com/copyright-fair-use-and-how-it-works-for-online-images/.
2.   Ibid.
3.   Matthew Goings, *What Is Fair Use?*, https://copyrightalliance.org/faqs/what-is-fair-use/.
4.   Ibid.
5.   See Lucie Růžičková, *AI and Copyright: The Legal Landscape*, https://blog.apify.com/ai-copyright/.

Ben Franklin and the Printing Press
Original Photo taken by Carl Shank on the grounds of The Masonic Home
Elizabethtown, PA

Electronic Publishing

Creating E-Documents

*"When preparing the layout for an electronic document,
typeface selection should be a prime consideration."*
(*E-Documents & On-Screen Reading*, Monotype Newsletter)

Electronic Publishing (E-Publishing). Having come of age in the early 2000s, electronic publishing provides the writer a means to publish their work online without having to go through the task of print design. First appearing in the 1980s in the form of plain text emails sent to a subscriber via a mailing list, the first e-journal appeared in 1994.

In the years 1985–1995, a revolution took place in the printing world from analog to digital printing with CD-ROMs and PDFs. E-Publishing has become faster, cheaper and allows many people across the world to have instant access to books and articles, as well as multimedia presentations. While many people still prefer the feel and look of a printed book, electronic books are growing in popularity.

Common Electronic Publishing formats are EPUB, PDF, HTML and TXT. (See Chart Below) The Kindle Reader for Amazon also has its own proprietary format, called KPF. Kindle Package Format (KPF) is the successor to their old MOBI format. Both are proprietary formats created by KDP and specifically meant for displaying ebooks on Kindle devices. The KPF file is built when you use Kindle Create, another proprietary tool for formatting ebooks specifically for sale in Kindles stores. More broad distribution of electronic publishing materials need EPUB or PDF formatting.

EPUB is the open standard format developed by the International Digital Publishing Forum (IDPF). It is specifically designed for e-books and is widely supported by e-readers, tablets and smartphones. It is a responsive format, meaning that the text adjusts itself to fit the screen of the device being used. EPUB supports interactive features such as videos, animations and hyperlinks. It is an ideal format for e-books that contain multimedia content. Also, the content can be updated in real time, allowing users to have an up-to-date document without having to download a new book. EPUB, however, has certain inflexible strictures for font use, cover design, and table of contents (TOC) that need to be obeyed for EPUB publication. The formatting can be challenging and requires a significant investment of time and resources.

The **PDF format** is a file format system developed by Adobe Systems in the 1990s. It is a very popular format that preserves the formatting of the original document, including images, fonts and layout. PDF files can be read on almost any device, including desktop computers, laptops, tablets and smartphones. It has the advantage next to printed materials of being WYSWYG, or what you see is what you get, in terms of visual compatibility with the original text. PDF is popularly used for textbooks, business reports and where a lot of specialty fonts and images are employed. EPUB is the better format if the content is primarily distributed through e-readers. If the content, however, is on various platforms, including desktop computers and mobile devices, PDF is the better choice.

The **HTML format** is a markup language used to create web pages. HTML files can be used to create e-books that can be read on a variety of devices using a web browser. It is the format offered by Adobe InDesign on their Digital Publishing menu, giving a web address to the file created through InDesign. I have created calendars using this format that I have offered online to anyone interested. (See the BLOG on Calendars for 2024)

The **TXT format** is a simple text file format that can be used for e-books. TXT files do not support formatting or multimedia content and are often used for public domain books that have been digitized. TXT files can be read on almost any device using a text editor or e-reader app.

EPUB Design Basics (using Lulu.com parameters)
Lulu suggests using a word processor, like Microsoft Word or Google Docs,

for creating e-books. Just like designing a printed book, the first step is to finish writing and editing the book. Here, don't forget to proofread, or better, have someone else, proofread the final book. Don't worry about formatting, metadata, or the cover design until you have finalized the book's contents.

Give emphasis to the typography of your book, blowing up the title to an exaggerated size, and setting the text in a highly contrasting color to the background. Make sure the typeface is clear and easy to read, and conveys the genre of your book instantly. When you're creating a fixed layout EPUB be sure to choose a highly legible font and make the font size and leading (space between baselines) generous. (See the type samples below for some help.)

Thanks to Microsoft Word's style-based formatting, you can let Word do most of the work for you for an EPUB approved file. Using the standardized headings in Word, Heading 1 style is for the book title, Heading 2 style is for the chapter titles, and the content is the body or Normal style in Microsoft Word.

Never use the "Enter" key to create extra white space. Reflowable books, like EPUBs, do not have a page size. They show content based on your reader's screen size. Multiple line breaks may make your text appear not as intended on different devices.

Images need to be appropriately sized in JPEG or PNG format. No single image can be greater than 3.2 million pixels (total pixels = length in pixels x width in pixels). Indeed, Apple will not accept EPUB files that contain individual images greater than 5.6 million pixels. They need to be clear, high-quality and complete. They must be clearly readable and saved in RGB color format.

A Table of Contents (TOC) is required for EPUBs, but not your usual printed contents with page numbers. Get rid of those. Use Microsoft's heading styles to define what appears in your table of contents.

Hyperlinks need to be checked to make sure they work properly.

Front & Back Matter. The Front matter to the book includes a title page, copyright page, dedication and preface. Back matter can include an about the author page, glossary, and bibliography. Use an ISBN either your own or free from Lulu without any spaces between the numbers. These are to be added to the main text of the book before formatting for EPUB.

The copyright page comes after the title page in an EPUB. It must have accurate metadata and look something like this:

Copyright © 2023 YOUR NAME. All rights reserved.
Published by YOUR NAME/COMPANY NAME
ISBN 1234567891012

Cover Design. The file must contain front cover image only (spine and back cover images will be rejected). The color must be RGB. Cover image must be a flat, 2D image and sized correctly: 612 x 792 pixels and 72–300 pixels per inch resolution. Any references to pricing cannot be included. No advertisements or hyperlinks or mention on possible included elements, like CDs. The cover text must be English, using a standard Latin character set. The cover content cannot infringe upon another publisher's or artist's copyright on the same cover.

Some other notes from Lulu.com include — No truncated text and no overlapping of text and images. EPUB files with interactive elements are not accepted by Lulu. EPUB files with fillable areas (like fill-in-the-blanks) are not accepted. Illegal content is not accepted, including public domain content or repurposed Project Gutenberg content. Advertisements or prices are not allowed in EPUB content. Links to online retailers or booksellers are not allowed.

While the cost of a book as an EPUB instead of a print paperback or hardback is certainly low, the disadvantages for me as a specialty typographer, with articles and books that illustrate many different fonts, special characters, and settings are enormous. I definitely choose the PDF route, even with Lulu.com, and the print book options. Moreover, they distribute the book over a wide swath of booksellers and commercial sites, like Amazon and Barnes & Noble.

Electronic Publishing

Which Format?

Publishing Needs	EPUB	PDF	TXT
Electronic use	yes	yes	yes[1]
Many images	no	yes	no
Text heavy content	no	yes	yes[2]
Preserves original formatting	no	yes	no
Multimedia content	yes	no	no
Interactive features	yes	no	no
Hyperlinks	yes	yes	yes
Different fonts	no[3]	yes	no
Looks like printing	no	yes	no
Flowing/dynamic text	yes	no	yes
Good for tablets/phones	yes	yes?[4]	yes
Broad distribution	yes	yes	yes
Cover image strictures	yes[5]	no	N/A
Challenging to create	yes[6]	no	no

[1]TXT format often used for digitized public domain books.
[2]TXT electronic publishing is usually text only without any formatting.
[3]EPUB books and articles English only, Latin based fonts.
    No specialty characters or foreign fonts.
[4]PDF files can be read on tablets; harder on phones.
[5]Cover images strictures are demanding, hi-resolution JPGs,
    612 x 792 pixels at 72 - 150 dpi resolution. No back cover.
[6]Challenging because of international EPUB standards which must be
    strictly adhered to.

Useful e-Documents Fonts
Font History & Use

Amasis
Amasis Italic
Amasis Bold
Amasis Bold Italic
1234567890!@#$%&
e-Printing is the future!

Amasis is a slab serif design which has been drawn with a humanist approach, rather than the traditional geometric construction associated with this style of letter. The result is a typeface that has an affinity with the Ionics, although in character it belongs to the latter decades of the twentieth century. The Amasis italic fonts, rather than being sloped roman or cursive in nature, are related more to the Old Style italics. Amasis works particularly well in small sizes where readability is important. Amasis has proved excellent for use on low resolution printers and for facsimile transmissions. A Monotype font.

Bembo
Bembo Italic
Bembo Semibold
Bembo Bold
Bembo Extra Bold
1234567890!@#$%&
e-Printing is the future!

The origins of Bembo go back to one of the most famous printers of the Italian Renaissance, Aldus Manutius. In 1496, he used a new roman typeface to print the book de Aetna, a travelogue by the popular writer Pietro Bembo. This type was designed by Francesco Griffo, a prolific punchcutter who was one of the first to depart from the heavier pen-drawn look of humanist calligraphy to develop the more stylized look we associate with roman types today. In 1929, Stanley Morison and the design staff at the Monotype Corporation used Griffo's roman as the model for a revival type design named Bembo. They made a number of changes to the fifteenth-century letters to make the font more adaptable to machine composition. The italic is based on letters cut by the Renaissance scribe Giovanni Tagliente. Because of their quiet presence and graceful stability, the lighter weights of Bembo are popular for book typography. The heavier weights impart a look of conservative dependability to advertising and packaging projects. With 31 weights, including small caps, Old style figures, expert characters, and an alternate cap R, Bembo makes an excellent all-purpose font family.

ITC Bookman Light
Bookman Medium
Bookman Medium Italic
Bookman Bold
Bookman Bold Italic
1234567890 !@#$%&
e-Printing is the future!

ITC Bookman font was designed by Edward Benguiat, whose goal was to design a typeface that had a clear resemblance to previous Bookman faces but was different and more versatile. This typeface retains all the traits of the original and adds a large x-height and moderate stroke contrast for optimal legibility. ITC Bookman font also has italics which are true cursive forms, as opposed to oblique roman characters.

Charter Roman
Charter Italic
Charter Bold
Charter Bold Italic
Charter Black & *Italic*
1234567890 !@#$%&
e-Printing is the future!

Charter was designed in the mid-1980s by Matthew Carter. The typeface was designed with the limitations of low- and middle-resolution output devices in mind; hence the squared off serifs and the economy of diagonals and curves. The design, however, became an instant success on its own merits. It is an excellent everyday typeface for a wide variety of uses including books and technical manuals. Charter offers small cap, extension and alternate typographer sets that help to make it more versatile and functional. ITC bought the Charter designs in 1993, but Bitstream retained the right to sell the original designs.

Useful e-Documents Fonts
Font History & Use

Dante
Dante Italic
Dante Bold
Dante Bold Italic
DANTE TITLING
1234567890!@#$%&
e-Printing is the future!

Dante was designed by Giovanni Mardersteig. Mardersteig started work on Dante after the Second World War when printing at the Officina Bodoni returned to full production. He drew on his experience of using Monotype Bembo and Centaur to design a new book face with an italic which worked harmoniously with the roman. Originally hand-cut by Charles Malin, Dante was adapted for mechanical composition by Monotype in 1957. The new digital font version has been re drawn, by Monotype's Ron Carpenter, free from any restrictions imposed by hot metal technology. The Dante font family was issued in 1993 in a range of three weights with a set of titling capitals. Dante is a beautiful book face which can also be used to good effect in magazines, periodicals etc.

Franklin Gothic
Franklin Gothic Italic
Franklin Gothic Medium
Franklin Gothic Bold
Franklin Gothic Bold Italic
Franklin Goth Heavy
Franklin Gothic Black
Franklin Gothic Ultra
1234567890!@#$%&
e-Printing is the future!

By 1915, all the major foundries offered families of sans serifs, sometimes called Gothic in the USA. Franklin was a response suitable for countries in the vanguard of the machine age. Designed by Morris Benton in 1903-1912, Franklin has preserved its own personality ever since. The ITC Franklin Gothic font family is a redrawing by ITC that keeps the original strength intact, meeting the demand for a strong typeface. ITC Franklin Gothic is better read in display sizes and considered a standard in the newspaper and advertising fields. URW Type Company.

Gill Sans Regular
Gill Sans Italic
Gill Sans Bold
Gill Sans Bold Italic
Gill Sans Condensed Bold
1234567890!@#$%&
e-Printing is the future!

The successful Gill Sans® was designed by the English artist and type designer Eric Gill and issued by Monotype in 1928 to 1930. The roots of Gill Sans can be traced to the typeface that Gill's teacher, Edward Johnston, designed for the signage of the London Underground Railway in 1918. Gill's alphabet is more classical in proportion and contains what have become known as his signature flared capital R and eyeglass lowercase g. Gill Sans is a humanist sans serif with some geometric touches in its structures. It also has a distinctly British feel. Legible and modern though sometimes cheerfully idiosyncratic, the lighter weights work for text, and the bolder weights make for compelling display typography.

Haarlemmer Regular
1234567890 !@#$&%
e-Printing is the future!

Haarlemmer is a recreation of a never-produced Jan Van Krimpen typeface that goes one step beyond authentic: it shows how he wanted it to be designed in the first place. The original, drawn in the late 1930s, was created for the Dutch Society for the Art of Printing and Books and was to be used to set a new edition of the Bible, using Monotype typesetting. Hence the problem: fonts for metal typesetting machines like the Linotype and Monotype had to be created within a crude system of predetermined character width values. Every letter had to fit within and have its spacing determined by a grid of only 18 units. Often, the italic characters had to share the same widths as those in the roman design. Van Krimpen believed this severely impaired the design process. The invasion of Holland in World War II halted all work on the Bible project, and the original Haarlemmer never went into production. Flash forward about sixty years. Frank E. Blokland, of The Dutch Type Library, wanted to revive the original Haarlemmer, but this time as Van Krimpen would have intended. Blokland reinterpreted the original drawings and created a typeface that matched, as much as possible, Van Krimpen's initial concept. full suite of small caps and old style figures. Van Krimpen would be proud.

Mundo Sans 100
Mundo Sans 500
Mundo Sans 500 Italic
Mundo Sans Regular
1234567890 !@#$%&
e-Printing is the future!

Mundo Sans, by Carl Crossgrove for the Monotype Studio, is distinctive, approachable – and ready to tackle jobs both big and small. Its open counters and large x-height, which give the design a straight-forward no-nonsense mien, are softened by inviting calligraphic undertones. With 10 weights and a complementary suite of cursive italics, there is little outside the range of the Mundo Sans family. The light weights are elegant in packaging and brochure design, the medium are easy readers in digital blogs and print periodicals and the bold command attention in banners and headlines. Mundo Sans is at home in a wide range of sizes, and comfortable in everything from wayfinding to mobile apps. Mundo Sans takes on complicated branding projects with efficient grace. The family enables companies and products to express their brand seamlessly in websites, advertising, corporate messaging, packaging – virtually everywhere visible engagement is possible

Nimrod Regular
Nimrod Cyr
Nimrod Cyr Inclined
1234567890 !@#$%&
e-Printing is the future!

An extremely versatile, intelligently restrained design by Robin Nicholas for Monotype in 1980. It works very well at small sizes thanks to its large x-height, sturdy serifs, and lack of ornament; yet it is not characterless. Nimrod has been used successfully in national newspapers and books. (The Guardian, London, from its late-1980s redesign until it was replaced by a Carter interpretation of Miller in 1998; the Concise Oxford English Dictionary in the typographically unsurpassed 1990 edition.)

Ocean Sans Book
Ocean Sans Book Semiextended
Ocean Sans Book Italic
Ocean Sans Semibold
OC Semibold Extended
Ocean Sans Bold
Ocean Sans Extra Bold
OC Extra Bold Extended
1234567890 !@#$%&
e-Printing is the future!

Released in 1993, Ocean Sans is a sans serif design created for Monotype by the talented Malaysian designer, Ong Chong Wah. The Ocean Sans font family has a distinct contrast between thick and thin strokes which sets it apart from the rather austere Grotesques with their more monotone appearance. Ocean Sans italic is an unusual design for a sans face, a strong cursive influence gives it a flowing rhythm not generally associated with sans serif italics. Ideal for text and display setting, the freshness of the Ocean Sans font family will give the user further scope in the design of catalogues, brochures, advertisements and flyers.

Useful e-Documents Fonts
Font History & Use

Plantin Regular
Plantin Italic
Plantin Semibold
Plantin Semibold Italic
Plantin Bold
1234567890 !@#$%&
e-Printing is the future!

Plantin is a Renaissance Roman as seen through a late–industrial-revolution paradigm. Its forms aim to celebrate fine sixteenth century book typography with the requirements of mechanized typesetting and mass production in mind. How did this anomalous design come about? In 1912 Frank Hinman Pierpont of English Monotype visited the Plantin-Moretus Museum in Antwerp, returning home with "knowledge, hundreds of photographs, and a stack of antique typeset specimens including a few examples of Robert Granjon's." Together with Fritz Stelzer of the Monotype Drawing Office, Pierpont took one of these overinked proofs taken from worn type to use as the basis of a new text face for machine composition. Body text set in Plantin produces a dark, rich texture that's suited to editorial and book work, though it also performs its tasks on screen with ease. Its historical roots lend the message it sets a sense of gravity and authenticity. The family covers four text weights complete with italics, with four condensed headline styles and a caps-only titling cut.

ITC Slimbach Book
Slimbach Book Italic
Slimbach Medium
Slimbach Medium Italic
Slimbach Bold
Slimbach Bold Italic
Slimbach Black
Slimbach Black Italic
1234567890 !@#$%&
e-Printing is the future!

ITC Slimbach font is the work of California calligrapher and type designer Robert Slimbach. Inspired in part by German fonts and the work of Hermann Zapf, Slimbach created a "contemporary text font with a progressive look", combining clean serif shapes with the warmth of calligraphic forms.

(Font information courtesy of myfonts.com and "e-Documents & On-Screen Reading" from *Monotype Newsletter*)

On-Screen Design Tips
- Choose a font with a tall x-height and open counters
- Increase the point size and open up the line spacing
- Use black text, when possible
- Limit the amount of content per line
- Ensure your font licenses cover your distribution plans

Creating Fillable Forms

Modern Form Making

"No one becomes a graphic designer because it
is their dream to design forms. But when you're a graphic designer,
you will inevitably have to design some forms. And forms are important.
Just ask Al Gore."
(*The Type Project Book*)

E veryone uses a form, whether it is a doctor's form, or an insurance form, or a credit form or a school registration form. Form creating is both an art and science. You want a form to be readable, convey the required information and be understandable. We also want forms, if they are online, to be fillable, with fields that invite the applicant to simply click and type in the information requested. Three programs that I use to create forms are the Adobe InDesign layout program, Acrobat, and Google Forms. Each has their strengths and weaknesses.

InDesign Form Making[1]

InDesign provides a path in the program for creating forms in their Button and Forms library. This is found in Windows > Interactive > Buttons and Forms which has form elements that you can use in designing your form. You can add simple form elements such as text fields, radio buttons, check boxes or signatures. You can also add actions to submit the form by email or print.

Solid strokes and fills to the form fields, on/off hover states for buttons, check boxes and radio buttons can be added. You can specify font and font sizes in text input fields. You can then export this simple form to Adobe Acrobat for additional editing. See Adobe's Help Index on forms for more information.

What is not told is that you must *actually create the form* and then add the buttons and field boxes and so forth. A very helpful tool is to use **InDesign Form Templates**, which professional designers have provided for our use. These are beautifully constructed forms that can be opened in Adobe Illustrator and used in programs like InDesign. I have included four downloaded forms below to show you the capabilities of such designed elements.

The advantages of using a high end program like InDesign are many for form creation. Like any other professional layout program, InDesign has all the bells and whistles that you need to design a form of your liking. Its myriad font selections, color selections, design elements and so forth will help you create an attractive and eye-catching form that is unlike many of the standard line forms you have seen. Many people also use Adobe Illustrator for form creation as well. The Form templates offered by Brand Packs are visually compelling and created for everything from registration forms to medical forms. Note the examples below.

The disadvantages are also to be noted. InDesign and the Forms Templates are not cheap. The InDesign program itself comes usually as part of the package of Creative Cloud from Adobe and costs over $50 per month for a subscription, which is the only way the current InDesign program is available. You cannot buy a current stand-alone InDesign program. The last stand alone program was in the CS series, InDesign CS 6, which is not available from Adobe any more.

Form Templates created for Adobe Creative Cloud are also available for a price, *brandpacks.com* offer seventeen outstanding InDesign compatible forms. They are available in the Adobe Stock program for a monthly fee of $30 – $200 per month, which includes not merely forms but all of the Adobe assets. One time users can retrieve five professionally made forms for $50 up to 150 forms and other assets for whopping price of $1,200. This fee is in addition to the regular Creative Cloud program fee. Additionally, extra type styles can be costly, since using these fonts come with licenses for which often you pay a fee.

Acrobat Forms

One of the most used programs for creating forms is Adobe Acrobat. Editable PDF forms are available using Acrobat to securely secure data from customers and clients, vendors and more. Using Acrobat's "tool bar," fillable form fields, text fields, drop down menus, checkboxes and signature fields are available. You can either download a paper form from your scanner or from a file on your computer. Acrobat then adds fillable form fields which you can then distribute. (See Sample Below)

The steps are fairly easy —

(1)   Open Acrobat

(2)   Click on the "Tools" tab and select "Prepare Form."

(3)   Select a file or scan a document

(4)   Acrobat will automatically analyze your document and add form fields.

(5)   Add new form fields:

(6)   Use the top toolbar and adjust the layout using tools in the right pane.

(7)   Save your fillable PDF:

You can also share it with others or click Distribute to collect responses automatically. (See https://helpx.adobe.com/acrobat/using/create-form.html for more help.)

However, unlike InDesign's or Illustrator's many layout elements, Acrobat depends on forms that have been already created for those professional touches.

Google Forms

Certainly, one of the easiest and cheapest way to create and use a form is through Google Forms, available at forms.google.com or your Google Drive. Many users have Google Drive enabled on their computers. There are a few Form Templates offered. (See Illustration below).

Step 1: Go to forms.google.com or Google Drive.

Step 2: Select a template.

Step 3: Change the title of your form.

Step 4: Adjust questions and answers.

Step 5: Customize the Google Form theme.

Step 6: Preview your form.

Google notes that you can add a header image and customize the color scheme and fonts used. Google offers this advice —

When you're done, simply click the Send button, and choose to send it via email (either a link to the form or the entire form embedded in an email), copy a link to share manually, or embed the form as HTML on your site. When the responses start trickling in, you can see them in a list of aggregated data or individually, along with a collection of charts appropriate to the question type. If you're a spreadsheet wizard, you can take this data to Google Sheets and look for deeper connections there."

In addition to that Sheets integration, you can also pre-fill a form to save your respondents some time, collaborate with others on your form, and browse a collection of add-ons on the Google Workspace Marketplace. Bonus: if your respondents are Google users, their progress will be saved on any given form for a month, so they can click away and come back to it later." (https://support. google.com/docs/answer/6281888?hl=en&co=GENIE.Platform %3DDesktop#zippy=%2Ccreate-a-form-from-google-drive)

Takeaways

As an avid InDesign user and typographer I tend toward using that platform for designing and using forms. Just to note that many of my colleagues use Adobe Illustrator, and that is all fine. I like the creative freedom, the outstanding visual appeal possible and the end results seen and appreciated.

I understand, however, the cost may be prohibitive for some, and busy office professionals may simply want a quick and easy form for their company. Google Forms cannot be beat with Adobe Acrobat coming in a close second. Take a look at the included forms below to get some ideas. If you would like CARE Typography to design your next form, let us know at *cshanktype@gmail.com*. We would be happy to quote you a price and offer a quick no-hassle turnaround.

1. An excellent InDesign form resource is found in Nigel French & Hugh D'Andrade, "Form Design," *The Type Project Book* (Pearson Education, 2021), 154–157.)

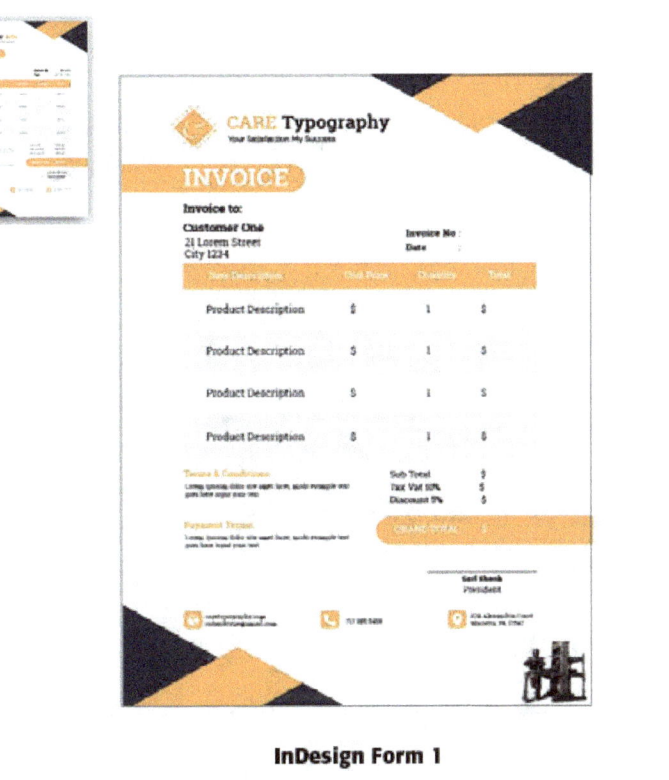

InDesign Form 1

InDesign Forms 1 & 2
PROs
- Use of InDesign Templates
- Allows wide-ranging design elements
- Multiple fonts and color schemes
- Can be made interactive for use online
- Can export to Acrobat for further use

CONs
- Costly for minimal use
- Requires knowledge of InDesign & layout procedures and time
- Specialty Fonts may also require purchase

Like other InDesign layout options, the "Forms" option (Window > Interactive > Button and Forms) allows the user to specify interactive elements which can then be used in online forms. On the above form, the logo was specially colored and substituted for the default logo. The Roboto Slab font was part of Adobe's type library. The bottom right corner image is from a Photoshop enhanced photo taken on the grounds of the Masonic Home in Elizabethtown, PA. The generic form was downloaded free from InDesign form templates for Adobe Illustrator.

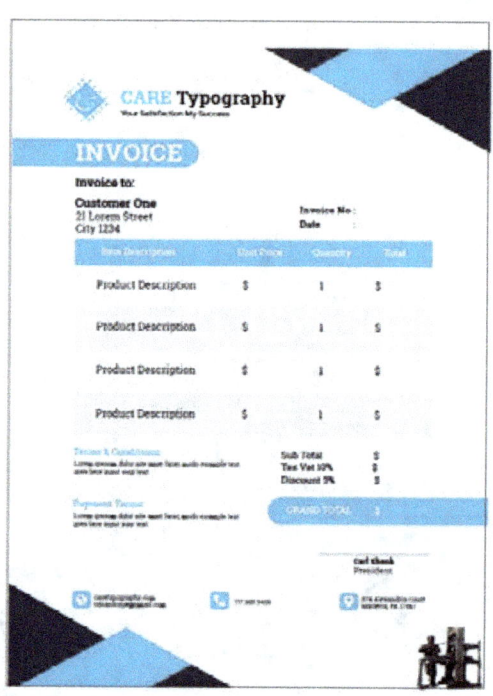

InDesign Form 2

InDesign Forms 1 & 2

PROs

- Use of InDesign Templates
- Allows wide-ranging design elements
- Multiple fonts and color schemes
- Can be made interactive for use online
- Can export to Acrobat for further use

CONs

- Costly for minimal use
- Requires knowledge of InDesign & layout procedures and time
- Specially Fonts may also require purchase

Like other InDesign layout options, the "Forms" option (Window > Interactive > Button and Forms) allows the user to specify interactive elements which can then be used in online forms. On the above form, the logo was specially colored and substituted for the default logo. The Roboto Slab font was part of Adobe's type library. The bottom right corner image is from a Photoshop enhanced photo taken on the grounds of the Masonic Home in Elizabethtown, PA. The generic form was downloaded free from InDesign form templates for Adobe Illustrator.

Cake Order Form

ORDER DATE :	PROMISE DATE :

CUSTOMER INFO	
NAME :	
EMAIL :	PHONE :
ADDRESS :	

FLAVOR	FILLING	ICING

ORDER DETAILS

DRAWING		SHAPE	

DELIVERY	LOCAL DROP OFF LOCAL PICK UP SHIPPING SHIP N. # SHIP DATE :	PAYMENT	Cash / Check Cashapp / Card PayPal / Other	Amount	SumTotal : Taxes : Shipping : Grandtotal :

Cake Order Form 1

Cake Forms 1 & 2

PROs

- Use of InDesign Templates
- Allows wide-ranging design elements
- Multiple fonts and color schemes
- Can be made interactive for use online
- Can export to Acrobat for further use
- Much of this form can be made in Acrobat
- A variation of the form can be made in Google Forms

CONs

- Costly for minimal use
- Requires knowledge of InDesign & layout kowledge and time
- Specialty graphics may require purchase or special permission

Like other InDesign layout options, the "Forms" option (Window > Interactive > Button and Forms) allows the user to specify interactive elements which can then be used in online forms. On the above form, the colorful header was downloaded for free from dreamstime.com. The generic form was downloaded from free InDesign form templates.

CAKE ORDER FORM

ORDER DATE		PROMISE DATE :	

CUSTOMER INFO

NAME :

EMAIL :   PHONE :

ADDRESS :

FLAVOR	ORDER DETAILS
FILLING	
ICING	

DRAWING	SHAPE	

Amount	PAYMENT	DELIVERY
LOCAL DROP OFF	Cash Check	SumTotal :
LOCAL PICK UP	Cashapp Card	Taxes :
SHIPPING		Shipping :
SHIP N. #	PayPal Other	Grandtotal :
SHIP DATE :		

Cake Order Form 2

Cake Forms 1 & 2

PROs

- Use of InDesign Templates
- Allows wide-ranging design elements
- Multiple fonts and color schemes
- Can be made interactive for use online
- Can export to Acrobat for further use
- Much of this form can be made in Acrobat
- A variation of the form can be made in Google Forms

CONs

- Costly for minimal use
- Requires knowledge of InDesign & layout kowledge and time
- Specialty graphics may require purchase or special permission

Like other InDesign layout options, the "Forms" option (Window > Interactive > Button and Forms) allows the user to specify interactive elements which can then be used in online forms. On the above form, the colorful font header was the Frosting BW Font from https://www.fontspace.com/frosting-bw-font-f79262 for personal use. The generic form was downloaded from free InDesign form templates.

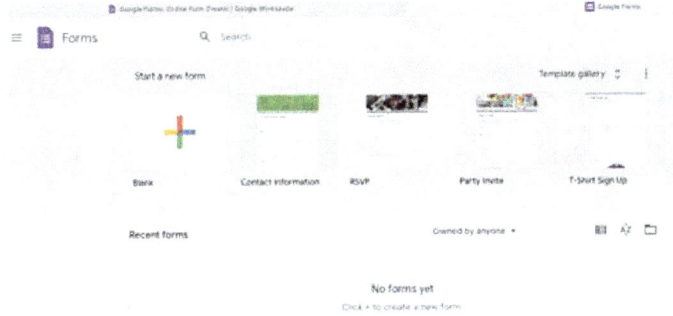

Google Forms Window

https://docs.google.com/forms/u/0/?tgif=d

Lincoln
Financial Group

The Lincoln National Life Insurance Company
PO Box 2340
Fort Wayne IN 46801-2340
Phone 800-4LINCOLN (800 454-6265)

Let's Keep in Touch

This form is used to keep a current record of your address for your annuity plan. This form should be filed with your other personal records. If you have a change of address, use this to notify Lincoln Life to update your business records. You can also contact us by calling 800 454-6265.

Old Address

Annuitant's name

Address

City, State, ZIP

New Address

Address

City, State, ZIP

Work phone no.

Signature

By signing below, you the annuitant, certify that you have read and understand this change of address notification. You also authorize Lincoln Life to update your name or address information on the contracts you indicate below.

Annuitant's signature   Date

List the contracts that need to be updated:

Acrobat Fillable Sample Form

Specialty Typography
Hour Glass Creation

"Dadaists were early 20th century avant-garde art typographers
who would use different fonts, turn them upside down, printing
horizontally, vertically and diagonally on the same page."
(Adapted from *The Type Project Book*)

Have you ever found something that challenged your creativity and skill? In typography such things exist all the time. In leafing through old ad booklets for the now defunct Adobe Minion Multiple Master Font (See CARE Typography Blogs on "More About Fonts" and "The Journey of Digital Type"), I found a challenging hour glass design with type expertly set within the hour glass to look like time slowly draining from top to bottom. That inspired me to see if I could do something similar with Adobe InDesign, which I love to use for all sorts of projects.

The challenge was to create an interior using only type that seems to be trickling down, as time is seen slowly moving down the hour glass. Since I am a Christian typographer, author and pastor, this was also an opportunity to pull from the Bible's perspective of time slowly drawing to a conclusion from the book of Revelation in the Bible. I chose Revelation 20 as the text to use inside the hour glass. I am certain that more professional illustrators and type setters can do a better job. But this is what I created using the tools and training in InDesign over the years.

Enjoy — and dive into your next type challenge!

The Hour Glass of Time

Then I saw an angel coming down from heaven, holding in his hand the key to the bottomless pit and a great chain. And he seized the dragon, that ancient serpent, who is the devil and Satan and bound him for a thousand years, and threw him into the pit and shut it and sealed it over him, so that he might not deceive the nations any longer, until the thousand years were ended. After that he must be released for a little while. Then I saw thrones, and seated on them were those to whom the authority to judge was committed. Also I saw the souls of those who had had been beheaded for the testimony of Jesus Jesus and for the word of God and tho who had not worshipped the beast or its image and had not received its mark on their foreheads or their hands. They came to life and reigned with Christ for a thousand years. The rest of the dead did not come to life until the thousand years were ended. Until the thousand ended, Satan will be released from his prison and will come out to deceive the nations that are at the of the earth, Gog and Magog, to gather them for battle is like the sand of the sea. And they marched up over

How Was It Done?

1. Scanned the original Adobe Hour Glass creation in their Minion Font ad booklet of the Minion Multiple Master font (1992). Also copied the text of Revelation 20:1–10 in the Bible in my Accordance program. Placed the text in a box outside of the document with the hour glass.
2. Used Adobe Photoshop to erase the original inner writing and outer decorative type. Saved the result as a GIF file with transparent background and pasted it in a 5.5 x 8.5 Adobe InDesign document.
3. Used "Layers" in Adobe InDesign and locked the hour glass GIF original on Layer 1.
4. Attempted to duplicate the sinking type in the upper part of the hour glass in a number of illustration programs, like Kitl. Unsuccessful. Also attempted to cut and use the "Paste Into" command in the edit section of InDesign, but that did not produce the sinking type filling.
5. With the "Pen" tool in InDesign and the "Type on a line" tool, drew individual curved lines from one side to the other of the hour glass top. This allows the image to look like it is draining from top to bottom. It also allows the type to look like it is bunching up at the bottom of the hour glass top.
6. Used regular type tool with scattered letters to indicate the dripping type.
7. Used "Paste Into" command to paste the last section in the bottom of the hour glass.
8. Traced the hour glass in Layer 2 using Adobe InDesign's "Pen" tool.
9. Imported a free Shutterstock photo (shutterstock_239 734942.jpg) to "Paste Into" the hour glass and then used the "Transparency" effect in InDesign to let the type show through.
10. Type used is Flat Brush Normal 18 pt for the title; Myriad Pro Regular 9 pt for the interior type.

Original Hour Glass AD by Adobe advertising their Minion Multiple Master Typeface back in 1992.

Helvetica's Better Substitutes

Upgrading Your Helvetica Uses

"As with all trends, Helvetica will someday
be back in style—in about two hundred years."
(Robin Williams, *Adobe Magazine*)

In the July/August 1995 edition of *Adobe Magazine*, Robin Williams, a noted typographer, says Helvetica, though immensely popular in the 60s and 70s, became passé. Like the beehive hairdo, Helvetica is continuously used but creates a tired and dated look. He says, "Just because it's on your computer doesn't mean you have to use it. The greatest single thing you could do for your publications is to invest in another sans serif ("without feet") face, one with a strong, bold black version in its family. As with all trends, Helvetica will someday be back in style—in about two hundred years."

He gives in another article some alternatives to Helvetica — ITC Franklin Gothic, Futura, Gill Sans and ITC Stone Sans as examples. And Daniel Will Harris in "Add Impact to Type" in the magazine *Technique*, March/April 1994 issue, suggests a wide range of alternatives to Helvetica — Agfa Roti's Sans, Avenue, Eras, Formata, Franklin Gothic, Frutiger, Gill Sans, ITC Goudy Sans, Lucida Sans, Optima, Shannon or Univers (some of these faces I do not have).

However, I find in hometown newspapers all over, that the tired and dated, and boring, use of Helvetica persists. In my hometown, a local printer, well-known and established for many years, uses Helvetica for ads that not only do not stand out, but fail in modern typographical terms. I am sure the rationale for Helvetica's use is that this is the typeface they have used for ages, is the most convenient, is the fastest to use on a compressed time factor, and no one has ever complained. However, there are typographical alternatives to Helvetica, even in a rather traditionally based hometown, that would give better results. I note them below with a copy of a typical printer set ad.

I fully understand that busy print shops and overworked staff, and perhaps not very well trained in modern typographical practices, simply default to Helvetica. But I believe we can all do better. Note the alternatives below and some information on the alternative typefaces used.

Helvetica Substitutes
The "Standards"

Standard Helvetica
ABCDEFGHIJKLMNOPQRSTUVWXYZ
ABCDEFGHIJKLMNOPQRSTUVWXYZ
abcdefghijklmnopqrstuvwxyz
1234567890

Formata
ABCDEFGHIJKLMNOPQRSTUVWXYZ
ABCDEFGHIJKLMNOPQRSTUVWXYZ
abcdefghijklmnopqrstuvwxyz
1234567890

Franklin Gothic
ABCDEFGHIJKLMNOPQRSTUVWXYZ
ABCDEFGHIJKLMNOPQRSTUVWXYZ
abcdefghijklmnopqrstuvwxyz
1234567890

Gill Sans
ABCDEFGHIJKLMNOPQRSTUVWXYZ
ABCDEFGHIJKLMNOPQRSTUVWXYZ
ABCDEFGHIJKLMNOPQRSTUVWXYZ
abcdefghijklmnopqrstuvwxyz
1234567890

Optima
ABCDEFGHIJKLMNOPQRSTUVWXYZ
ABCDEFGHIJKLMNOPQRSTUVWXYZ
abcdefghijklmnopqrstuvwxyz
1234567890

Futura
ABCDEFGHIJKLMNOPQRSTUVWXYZ
ABCDEFGHIJKLMNOPQRSTUVWXYZ
ABCDEFGHIJKLMNOPQRSTUVWXYZ
abcdefghijklmnopqrstuvwxyz
1234567890

Avenir
ABCDEFGHIJKLMNOPQRSTUVWXYZ
ABCDEFGHIJKLMNOPQRSTUVWXYZ
ABCDEFGHIJKLMNOPQRSTUVWXYZ
abcdefghijklmnopqrstuvwxyz
1234567890

Other Choices

Myriad Pro
ABCDEFGHIJKLMNOPQRSTUVWXYZ
ABCDEFGHIJKLMNOPQRSTUVWXYZ
abcdefghijklmnopqrstuvwxyz
1234567890

Lucida Sans
ABCDEFGHIJKLMNOPQRSTUVWXYZ
ABCDEFGHIJKLMNOPQRSTUVWXYZ
abcdefghijklmnopqrstuvwxyz
1234567890

AG Opus
ABCDEFGHIJKLMNOPQRSTUVWXYZ
ABCDEFGHIJKLMNOPQRSTUVWXYZ
abcdefghijklmnopqrstuvwxyz
1234567890

AquaticHeavy Black
ABCDEFGHIJKLMNOPQRSTUVWXYZ
abcdefghijklmnopqrstuvwxyz
1234567890

Bauhaus
ABCDEFGHIJKLMNOPQRSTUVWXYZ
ABCDEFGHIJKLMNOPQRSTUVWXYZ
ABCDEFGHIJKLMNOPQRSTUVWXYZ
abcdefghijklmnopqrstuvwxyz
1234567890

Benjamin
ABCDEFGHIJKLMNOPQRSTUVWXYZ
abcdefghijklmnopqrstuvwxyz
1234567890

LITHOS PRO
ABCDEFGHIJKLMNOPQRSTUVWXYZ
ABCDEFGHIJKLMNOPQRSTUVWXYZ
1234567890

Lato
ABCDEFGHIJKLMNOPQRSTUVWXYZ
ABCDEFGHIJKLMNOPQRSTUVWXYZ
abcdefghijklmnopqrstuvwxyz
1234567890

Masonic Village Hospice

Volunteers Needed

We are looking for volunteers to visit with patients
receiving hospice care in your local community.

Our next orientation is:

Wednesday, November 1st and
Thursday, November 2nd
8:00am-12:30pm
*You must attend both days.

Masonic Village Campus - Health Care Center
600 Freemason Drive, Elizabethtown

Registration closes one week before orientation.
Please call for more information and to reserve
your seat! (717) 367-1121 ext. 33024

Masonic Village Hospice

Volunteers Needed

Looking for volunteers to visit with patients
receiving hospice care in your community

Next orientation

Wednesday & Thursday
November 1 & 2*
8:00 AM – 12:30 PM

Masonic Village Campus | Health Care Center
600 Free Mason Drive, Elizabethtown

For reservations and more information
717.367.1121 ext. 33024

Registration closes one week before orientation
*Attendance at both days necessary

(TOP LEFT) Original Ad from local newspaper.

(TOP RIGHT) **My preference.** Ad redone with the Formata font. Clear and professional. Note the "AM" and "PM" small caps lettering.

(BOTTOM LEFT) Ad redone with Gill Sans font. UltraBold in the "Volunteers Needed" headline. Smaller Masonic Home logo used. More white space and easier to read.

(BOTTOM RIGHT) Ad redone with Lato font. Black emphasis in the "Volunteers Needed" headline. Smaller Masonic Home logo used. More white space and easier to read.

Masonic Village Hospice

Volunteers Needed

Looking for volunteers to visit with patients
receiving hospice care in your community

Next orientation

Wednesday & Thursday
November 1 & 2*
8:00 AM – 12:30 PM

Masonic Village Campus | Health Care Center
600 Free Mason Drive, Elizabethtown

For reservations and more information
717.367.1121 ext. 33024

Registration closes one week before orientation
*Attendance at both days necessary

Masonic Village Hospice

Volunteers Needed

Looking for volunteers to visit with patients
receiving hospice care in your community

Next orientation

Wednesday & Thursday
November 1 & 2*
8:00 AM – 12:30 PM

Masonic Village Campus | Health Care Center
600 Free Mason Drive, Elizabethtown

For reservations and more information
717.367.1121 ext. 33024

Registration closes one week before orientation
*Attendance at both days necessary

Masonic Village Hospice

Volunteers Needed

Looking for volunteers to visit with patients
receiving hospice care in your community

Next orientation

Wednesday & Thursday
November 1 & 2*
8:00 AM - 12:30 PM

Masonic Village Campus | Health Care Center
600 Free Mason Drive, Elizabethtown

For reservations and more information
717.367.1121 ext. 33024

Registration closes one week before orientation
*Attendance at both days necessary

Masonic Village Hospice

Volunteers Needed

Looking for volunteers to visit with patients
receiving hospice care in your community

Next orientation

Wednesday & Thursday
November 1 & 2*
8:00 AM - 12:30 PM

Masonic Village Campus | Health Care Center
600 Free Mason Drive, Elizabethtown

For reservations and more information
717.367.1121 ext. 33024

Registration closes one week before orientation
*Attendance at both days necessary

(TOP LEFT) Ad redone with the Futura font. Extra bold in the "Volunteers Needed" headline. Clear and professional. Note the "AM" and "PM" small caps lettering. Smaller Masonic logo.

(BOTTOM LEFT) Ad redone with Optima font, Extra Black emphasis in the "Volunteers Needed" headline. Smaller Masonic Home logo used. More white space and easier to read.

(TOP RIGHT) Ad redone with the Avenir Next font. Avenir Heavy in the "Volunteers Needed" headline. Clear and professional. Smaller Masonic logo.

(BOTTOM RIGHT) Ad redone with Myriad Pro font. Bold emphasis in the "Volunteers Needed" headline. Smaller Masonic Home logo used. More white space and easier to read.

Masonic Village Hospice

Volunteers Needed

Looking for volunteers to visit with patients
receiving hospice care in your community

Next orientation

Wednesday & Thursday
November 1 & 2*
8:00 AM – 12:30 PM

Masonic Village Campus | Health Care Center
600 Free Mason Drive, Elizabethtown

For reservations and more information
717.367.1121 ext. 33024

Registration closes one week before orientation
*Attendance at both days necessary

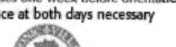

Masonic Village Hospice

Volunteers Needed

Looking for volunteers to visit with patients
receiving hospice care in your community

Next orientation

Wednesday & Thursday
November 1 & 2*
8:00 AM – 12:30 PM

Masonic Village Campus | Health Care Center
600 Free Mason Drive, Elizabethtown

For reservations and more information
717.367.1121 ext. 33024

Registration closes one week before orientation
*Attendance at both days necessary

About the Font Selections*

The Formata font – Bernd Möllenstädt's first type design, Formata, was released in 1984. Instead of linear severity common to many sans serifs, Formata offers curved strokes and interesting details that are subtle in smaller sizes but distinguishable in larger sizes, thus, appropriate for both text and display. The family has an extensive weight range complimented by small caps, old style figures, fractions and the Euro symbol for both the normal and condensed versions. The breadth of the family makes it an excellent choice for a wide range of applications from bodies of text, office memorandum, scanning and faxing documents to attention-grabbing headlines.

Gill Sans font — The successful Gill Sans® was designed by the English artist and type designer Eric Gill and issued by Monotype in 1928 to 1930. The roots of Gill Sans can be traced to the typeface that Gill's teacher, Edward Johnston, designed for the signage of the London Underground Railway in 1918. Gill's alphabet is more classical in proportion and contains what have become known as his signature flared capital R and eyeglass lowercase g. Gill Sans is a humanist sans serif with some geometric touches in its structures. It also has a distinctly British feel. Legible and modern though sometimes cheerfully idiosyncratic, the lighter weights work for text, and the bolder weights make for compelling display typography.

Lato font – Lato is a sans serif typeface family started in the summer of 2010 by Warsaw-based designer Łukasz Dziedzic ("Lato" means "Summer" in Polish). In December 2010 the Lato family was published under the Open Font License by his foundry tyPoland, with support from Google.

Futura font — Futura was designed for Bauer company in 1927 by Paul Renner. This is a sans serif face based on geometrical shapes, representative of the aesthetics of the Bauhaus school of the 1920s-30s. Issued by the Bauer Foundry in a wide range of weights and widths, Futura became a very popular choice for text and display setting. Originally Cyrillic version of eight styles was developed at ParaType (ParaGraph) in 1995 by Vladimir Yefimov. Additional Cyrillic styles were developed in 2007 by Isabella Chaeva. Simultaneously, the old eight styles were partly revised to match the whole family. Now the new Futura is an uniform type system, consisting of seven weights with corresponding obliques plus eight condensed styles. All these fonts are coordinated in letterforms, metrics, and weights to work better together.

Optima font — Although Optima is almost always grouped with sans serif typefaces, it should be considered a serifless roman. True to its Roman heritage, Optima has wide, full-bodied characters – especially in the capitals. Only the E, F and L deviate with narrow forms. Consistent with other Zapf designs, the cap S in Optima appears slightly top-heavy with a slight tilt to the right. The M is splayed, and the N, like a serif design, has light vertical strokes. The lowercase a and g in Optima are high-legibility two-storied designs. Optima can be set within a wide choice of line spacing values – from very tight to very open. In fact, there are few limits to the amount of white space that can be added between lines of text. Optima also benefits from a wide range of letter spacing capability. It can be set quite tight, or even slightly open – especially the capitals. If there are any guidelines, Optima should be set more open than tight. It's not that readability is affected that much when Optima is set on the snug side; it's just that the unhurried elegance and light gray typographic color created by the face are disrupted when letters are set too tight. Optima is also about as gregarious as a typeface can be.

Avenir font – Avenir Next Pro is a new take on a classic face– it's the result of a project whose goal was to take a beautifully designed sans and update it so that its technical standards surpass the status quo, leaving us with a truly superior sans family. This family is not only an update though, in fact it is the expansion of the original concept that takes the Avenir Next design to the next level. In addition to the standard styles ranging from UltraLight to Heavy, this 32-font collection offers condensed faces that rival any other sans on the market in on and off–screen readability at any size alongside heavy weights that would make excellent display faces in their own right and have the ability to pair well with so many contemporary serif body types. Overall, the family's design is clean, straightforward and works brilliantly for blocks of copy and headlines alike.

Akira Kobayashi worked alongside Avenir's esteemed creator Adrian Frutiger to bring Avenir Next Pro to life. It was Akira's ability to bring his own finesse and ideas for expansion into the project while remaining true to Frutiger's original intent, that makes this not just a modern typeface, but one ahead of its time.

Myriad Pro font — Designed by Robert Slimbach and Carol Twombly from Adobe, Myriad is one of the Adobe Original fonts available. First released in 1992, Myriad has become popular for both text and display composition. As an OpenType release, Myriad Pro expands this sans serif family to include Greek and Cyrillic glyphs, as well as adding oldstyle figures and improving support for Latin-based languages.

(*Font Selection information provided by myfonts.com and Adobe)

A Type Tool and An Offer
A Very Usable Typography Tool

I remember the "good old days" of type and typesetting and layout tools mailed to you by different companies. I still have many of those type spec tools in my layout drawer. I have constructed a Type Tool for your use and enjoyment. It has been a labor of love, constructing the inch ruler, centimeter ruler and pica & point rulers. These have been done from hand by using standard measuring tools. I also put on a fractional equivalency chart, a useful dingbats reference, and two inside pull sliders giving some samples of popular font choices and amazing ampersands.

I am including the construction method of this Tool below for your use and fun. You will need a program that can produce an 11 x 8.5 image and download the PDF from my online site at *caretypography.com*.

I am also offering through our Store the Type Tool, a thumb drive of all the blogs I have posted up to this date, and a neat bookmark. This book was made out of those online blogs. Quite a bit of work went into these instruments of typography and graphic design tools, so I hope you are able to order and use them freely. They are copyrighted, so please do not remake them as your own.

For those of you who purchase this book, the ***Type Tool and thumb drive are FREE!*** Simply email me at cshanktype@gmail.com.

Most of all, enjoy!

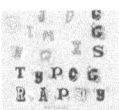 February 21, 2023

Type Tool

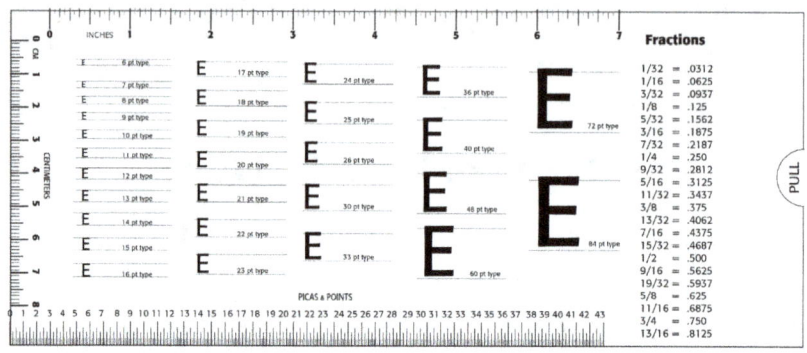

Fractions

1/32	=	.0312
1/16	=	.0625
3/32	=	.0937
1/8	=	.125
5/32	=	.1562
3/16	=	.1875
7/32	=	.2187
1/4	=	.250
9/32	=	.2812
5/16	=	.3125
11/32	=	.3437
3/8	=	.375
13/32	=	.4062
7/16	=	.4375
15/32	=	.4687
1/2	=	.500
9/16	=	.5625
19/32	=	.5937
5/8	=	.625
11/16	=	.6875
3/4	=	.750
13/16	=	.8125

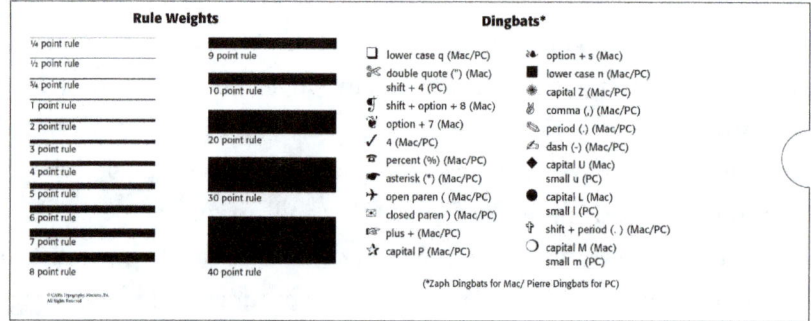

TYPE TOOL (Back)

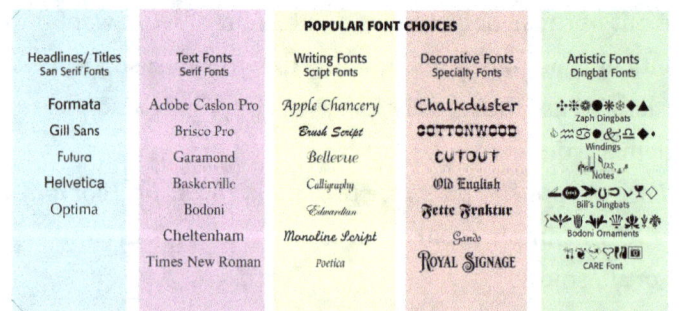

Interior One Side One

Beautiful Ampersands

- Garamond Italic
- Minion Italic
- Jenson Pro Italic
- Baskerville Italic
- Caslon Pro Italic
- Apple Chancery
- Buffjust
- Book Antiqua Italic
- Co021n Italic
- ITC Stone Sans Italic
- Limited Roman
- Brioso Pro Italic
- Zapf Chancery

Interior One Side Two

Display Fonts

This is Formata Bold 12 pt.
This is Formata Regular 12 point
This is Formata Italic 12 point

This is Gill Sans Bold 12 point
This is Gill Sans Regular 12 point
This is Gill Sans Italic 12 point

This is Futura Bold 12 point
This is Futura Medium 12 point
This is Futura Italic 12 point

This is Helvetica Bold 12 point
This is Helvetica Regular 12 point
This is Helvetica Oblique 12 point

This is Optima Bold 12 point
This is Optima Extra Black 12 point
This is Optima Regular 12 point
This is Optima Italic 12 point

Text Font Samples

This is Adobe Caslon Pro, 12 point, set on 14.4
point leading. A nice text font for general use. You
can see the usability.
ABCDEFGHIJKLMNOPQRSTUVWXYZ
abcdefghijklmnopqrstuvwxyz
1234567890 = + @#$%^&*'()

This is Brisco Pro Regular, 12 point, set on 14.4 point
leading. A nice text font for general use. You can see
the usability.
ABCDEFGHIJKLMNOPQRSTUVWXYZ
abcdefghijklmnopqrstuvwxyz
1234567890 = + @#$%^&*'()

This is Garamond Premier Pro Regular, 12 point, set
on 14.4 point leading. A nice text font for general use.
You can see the usability.
ABCDEFGHIJKLMNOPQRSTUVWXYZ
abcdefghijklmnopqrstuvwxyz
1234567890 = + @#$%^&*'()

PULL

Interior Two Side One

Text Font Samples

This is Baskerville Regular, 12 point, set on 14.4
point leading. A nice text font for general use. You
can see the usability.
ABCDEFGHIJKLMNOPQRSTUVWXYZ
abcdefghijklmnopqrstuvwxyz
1234567890 = + @#$%^&*'()

This is Bodoni Book, 12 point, set on 14.4 point
leading. A nice text font for general use. You can see
the usability.
ABCDEFGHIJKLMNOPQRSTUVWXYZ
abcdefghijklmnopqrstuvwxyz
1234567890 = + @#$%^&*'()

This is Cheltenham Book, 12 point, set on
14.4 point leading. A nice text font for general
use. You can see the usability.
ABCDEFGHIJKLMNOPQRSTUVWXYZ
abcdefghijklmnopqrstuvwxyz
1234567890 = + @#$%^&*'()

This is Times New Roman Regular, 12 point, set
on 14.4 point leading. A nice text font for general
use. You can see the usability.
ABCDEFGHIJKLMNOPQRSTUVWXYZ
abcdefghijklmnopqrstuvwxyz
1234567890 = + @#$%^&*'()

This is Arno Pro Regular, 12 point, set on 14.4 point
leading. A nice text font for general use. You can see the
usability.
ABCDEFGHIJKLMNOPQRSTUVWXYZ
abcdefghijklmnopqrstuvwxyz
1234567890 = + @#$%^&*'()

Interior Two Side Two

Making Your Own Type Tool

Use heavy stock 8½ x 11 paper and a good color laser (or ink jet) printer that prints all the way to the edge of the paper. (If you shrink the diagram to "fit" the normal printing on a letter size paper, the rulers will not be accurate.)

STEP 1 – Trim off the top trim piece of the TOOL so that the top edge of the INCH Ruler is at the top of the final piece.

STEP 2 – Trim side piece with the cut outs. Trim the cut outs last.

STEP 3 – Trim the "Detach" Piece. Follow the line carefully so that you do not trim off the side FOLD piece.

STEP 4 – Using a thin straight edge, FOLD inside the bottom ¼ inch piece.

STEP 5 – FOLD in the tab piece on the left.

STEP 6 – Carefully FOLD the entire piece in the middle so that the bottom edge of the PICA & POINTS ruler is at the bottom of the final folded piece and the top edge of the INCH Ruler lines up at the top perfectly.

STEP 7 – TRIM the cut outs, making a perfect semi-circle opening.

STEP 8 – Use a little glue to glue the top and side tabbed pieces. Be careful not to get glue on the main interior of the Type Tool.

STEP 9 – Using the Guide Lines, trim the Interior Slide. This is a two-sided piece. Trim a bit off the interior corners to help the slide move in and out of the Type Tool.

You can use heavy paper stock for this project. A sharp utility knife and metal straight edge will help in the process, as well as a one inch Circle Punch for the cut outs and a Scoring Tool for the folds.

You can also purchase this Type Tool from our Store at *caretypography.com.*

Enjoy!

Bookmark

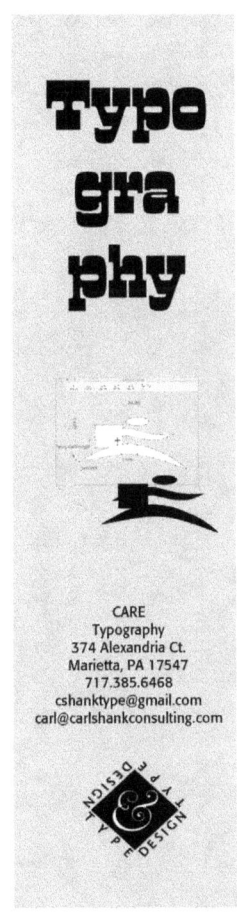

Selected Bibliography

Beaumont, Michael. *Type: Design, Color, Character & Use.* Cincinnati: Quarto Publishing, 1987 and 1991.

Bergsland, David. *Practical Font Design With FontLab 5.* Mankato, Minnesota: Radiqx Press, 2016. Kindle Edition.

Bertrand, J. Mark. "A Revolution in Bible Design." *Bible Study Magazine,* (November/December 2021).

Brady, Philip. *Using Type Right: 121 Basic No-Nonsense Rules for Working With Type.* Cincinnati: North Light, 1988.

Bringhurst, Robert. *The Elements of Typographic Style.* Vancouver, BC: Hartley & Marks, 1992, 1996, 2004, 2005.

Franklin Covey Style Guide: For Business and Technical Communication. Franklin Covey Co., 1994 and 1999.

French, Nigel & D'Andrade, Hugh. *The Type Project Book: Typographic Projects to Sharpen Your Creative Skills & Diversify Your Portfolio.* San Francisco, CA: Pearson Education, Inc., New Riders, 2021.

Harris, Daniel Will. "Add Impact With Type," *Technique,* Mar/Apr, 1994.

McClelland and Danuloff, Craig. *Desktop Publishing Type & Graphics: A Comprehensive Handbook.* Harcourt Brace Jovanovich, 1987.

McWade, John. *Before & After: How To Design Cool Stuff.* Vol. 1 No. 2 (1990), Vol. 2 No. 2 (1991), Vol. 4 No. 3 (1994), Vol. 4 No 4 (1995), Vol. 4 No. 5 (1995). Out of print.

Moye, Stephen. *Fontographer: Type by Design.* MIS Press, 1995.

Parker, Roger C. *Looking Good in Print: A Guide to Basic Design for Desktop*

Publishing. Chapel Hill, NC, 1988.

Silver, Linda, ed. *Print's Best Letterheads & Business Cards 4: Winning Designs from Print Magazine's National Competition.* New York: RC Publications Inc., 1995.

"Sixth Annual Type Issue," *Adobe Magazine,* Vol. 6, No. 4 (March/April 1995). Formerly *Aldus Magazine.* Out of Print.

White, Alex. *How To Spec Type.* New York: Watson-Guptill Pub., Roundtable Press, 1987.

Williams, Robin. "Thirteen Telltale Signs," *Adobe Magazine,* July/August, 1995.

And many online sources noted in the various articles.

www.ingramcontent.com/pod-product-compliance
Lightning Source LLC
Chambersburg PA
CBHW060414290526
45791CB00002B/751